UNAPOLOGETICALLY
MAGICK

ABOUT THE AUTHOR

Whiskey Stevens (Ontario, Canada) is actively involved in many witchcraft communities, including DIY Witches; Witches of Ontario; Spells, Herbs, Oils: Witchcraft 101; and Tarot Professionals Group. Her writing has been featured in *Witch Way*, *The Witch*, and *Witchology*. She is also a death doula and runs a popular YouTube channel.

Foreword by Devin Hunter

UNAPOLOGETICALLY
MAGICK

STANDING STRONG AT THE
CENTER OF YOUR WITCHCRAFT

Author of *Rise of the Witch*

WHISKEY STEVENS

LLEWELLYN PUBLICATIONS
Woodbury, Minnesota

FIRST EDITION
First Printing, 2023

Book design by Christine Ha
Cover design by Kevin R. Brown

Llewellyn Publications is a registered trademark of Llewellyn Worldwide Ltd.

Library of Congress Cataloging-in-Publication Data (Pending)
ISBN: 978-0-7387-7001-7

Llewellyn Publications
A Division of Llewellyn Worldwide Ltd.
2143 Wooddale Drive
Woodbury, MN 55125-2989
www.llewellyn.com

Printed in the United States of America

OTHER BOOKS BY WHISKEY STEVENS

Rise of the Witch: Making Magick Happen Your Way

CONTENTS

List of Exercises ... xi
Disclaimer ... xiii
Foreword by Devin Hunter ... xv
Introduction ... 1

Chapter 1: What Is Magick? ... 5

Chapter 2: Waking the Inner Child ... 11

Chapter 3: Your Path Is Not for Everybody ... 29

Chapter 4: Everyday Alchemy ... 47

Chapter 5: Tarot Royalty ... 79

Chapter 6: Everyday Magick ... 103

Chapter 7: Alchemy of Appearance ... 115

Chapter 8: Magickal Record Keeping ... 135

Chapter 9: The Art of Language ... 151

Chapter 10: Magickal Living: Things to Consider ... 159

Chapter 11: Digital Magick ... 171

Chapter 12: Confronting Your Own Programming ... 191

Chapter 13: Personal Power ... 203

Conclusion ... 209
References ... 213

EXERCISES

Creating Your Map... 17

Grounding... 21

Believing in Your Magick... 22

Tarot Meditation... 35

Two Fools Meditation... 38

Tapping Into Your Emotions for Spellwork... 55

Clearing the Energy... 58

Calling Forth Emotions... 59

Good Luck Talisman... 61

Tapping Into the Idea Highway... 66

Alchemizing Your Birth Chart... 72

Tarot Walk Through... 74

Royalty Ritual... 89

Journaling with the Royals... 95

Making a Royal Decision... 99

Daily Empowerment... 107

Create Your Book of Muse... 119

Create a Magickal Talisman... 123

Self-Love Meditation... 127

Glamour Spell for Confidence... 130

Check-in Journal Prompt... 160

Creating a Digital Egregore... 175
Creating a Digital Servitor... 178
File Housing for Digital Servitor... 181
Creating a Money Servitor... 183
Money Visualization... 185
Blooming Energy Meditation... 207

DISCLAIMER

This book and the contents herein are not meant to be a substitute for any medical care and do not substitute the use of a licensed physician, counselor, or therapist. Any herbs or other ingredients used in the exercises should be carefully considered, and prior to use, you should consult with your medical professional. The author and the publisher are not responsible for any misuse of the material. Take precautions, be prepared, and use proper judgment before attempting anything.

Foreword

THE COST OF ADMISSION

By Devin Hunter

As I sat at my desk staring at the blinking text bar on the open tab, I remember thinking to myself, "I can't write this. People are going to think I am a nutcase. I will never be able to get a normal job again because all an employer will have to do is google my name and see that I am the guy who encourages people to talk to the voices in their head. Nope. Uh-uh. This was a stupid idea."

In an eagerness to continue writing, I had, weeks before, signed the contract for my second book (*The Witch's Book of Spirits*) while riding the wave of excitement that came on the heels of publishing my first (*The Witch's Book of Power*). *At the time*, I was ready to take on the world and tell everyone about my magick. *At the time*, I felt like I was unstoppable. My publisher loved it, the readers loved it, and for a brief moment of sheer bliss, I was on top of the world. That version of me, some total jackass who had been living in a bubble of "I am going to be a professional author, and this is my calling," thought it was a fantastic idea to send in a proposal just days after I had sent in the final edits on my first. That version of me was having a very good day. Unfortunately, that version of me was unable to come to work when it came time to actually do the thing.

Instead, I had normal me. The socially awkward, emotionally squishy, overly critical guy with ADHD whose mind is haunted by lifelong memories of being the odd one out. Always the outsider even in a room full of outsiders. All too aware of what people do when people like me show just how weird we are. Was I really going to write a book that exposed my biggest secret: that I have talked to spirits since I can remember and have a familiar spirit who takes the shape of an owl? "It's pathetic, and anyone with an ounce of reason is going to laugh me out of existence. No one will ever take me seriously again."

After staring at that little blinking bar for what felt like hours without it moving, I gave up and properly recoiled into my stupor. I had resigned to the spiteful clarity of it all and surrendered to the idea of canceling the contract. *They* won. *They* weren't going to use my weirdness against me again. I wasn't going to give them the chance. I wasn't going to embarrass my family even more than I already had in the past. I grew up in a small town; everyone knew everyone's business. It wouldn't take long for them to find out, and with the way things usually went, there would be scandal.

"You're such a tool," said one of those little voices I was so afraid to write about. "The minute you send that email, you will be filled with regret, and you'll remember it for the rest of your life. This is what you wanted; this was always the plan."

"Yeah, but now, I won't be able to hide anymore." There it was. There was the truth. In all my brooding and depth that night, it was only then that I got to the bottom of the issue. I knew that statement was loaded with layers upon layers of nuance that all merged upon the same conclusion for one reason or another: I was scared for people to really see me, to know that I thought differently, acted differently than them. There I was, in my late twenties, far away from high school or the little gossipy town I grew up in, but I was still there in so many ways. The normal version of me was actually a fourteen-year-old gay witch boy hiding as many elements of his identity from the world as he could as a matter of survival.

"This is the cost of admission," the little voice continued. "It has always been the cost of admission."

I didn't need that explained. It is a phrase I use often with clients when we talk about their love lives. It's a metaphor for the ways we have to change when we love someone and the things we have to accept about who they are as part of loving them. If you want to ride the ride, you have to pay the cost of admission. In this case, the ride was my career, but the cost? The cost was, well, just being myself. Why was being myself so scary?

The truth is that I had been wanting to write that book for years, and I wanted very much to bring my voice to the topic. The only way I could do that was to talk about the things that made my take unique, which meant being open about who I was. The cost of admission for bringing my voice to the table was that I had to speak up regardless of what I thought might come as a potential outcome.

Other fears crept up too. The fear of people just hating it in general, or it not being accepted by my community of peers and readers. But there was always that little voice saying, "This is the cost of admission." To do what I wanted to do, to do that thing that I felt passionate about, I had to pay the cost. Otherwise, I was going to have to send that email to my editor.

The more I thought about it, the more I realized that I was the jackass. Why was I getting upset with that prior version of me who said yes when he was feeling good about doing the thing he loved? I was fortunate to be in this position at all, and he knew that and cherished it; that is why he said yes. Furthermore, honestly, who cares what people think back home or what my peers might think? I was finding myself coming to the conclusion that anyone who was in my shoes would be worried about the same things.

The fear, the anxiety, the pieces of my shadow that still remained from years of just wanting to fit in so I could be left alone vanished, and all that remained was my resolve to be myself. Because, dear reader, the cost I was paying, and had paid for years by not getting on the ride, was not doing the thing I loved and, ultimately, not loving myself enough to do it. So, I wrote the book.

A few years later, I had the privilege of having Whiskey Stevens on my show, *Modern Witch*. The plan was for us to talk about her latest book, but we ended up discussing our struggles with being writers and being authentic about who we are in our writing. She mentioned how awkward it feels to put yourself out there and to be open about what you do in your practice, and it triggered memories of me sitting there staring at that damn blinking bar. I felt a kinship to her instantly because in that moment she was my sister. I knew what she was talking about; we had both obviously had similar moments and had found our way through the other side—survivors of near self-sabotage at the hands of less-resilient versions of ourselves.

What came out of that conversation—which was fantastic by the way; go check it out—was the ultimate truth that it is hard to be yourself. It is hard to stand out. It is hard to take a risk. It is hard to tell people about your imaginary owl friend. And, most importantly, it is hard to get over the itty-bitty-shitty committee in the back of your head that tells you that you are stoppable. You aren't. You are unstoppable when you surrender to what you love, but that is easy to forget sometimes.

Luckily, we have Whiskey and her work to help alleviate the aches and pains that come with surrendering to that love. With *Unapologetically Magick*, she helps us perform triage on our inner child and shows us how to embrace our magick and the unique path it places us on. She teaches us how to fuse the great works of alchemy into a daily practice that allows us to confront our negative programing with magick and intention. And, while holding space for the vulnerable nature of this work, she helps us build tools that are unique to our lives so that we can succeed on our terms. The best part is that she does this all with a thoroughly modern approach that helps us remain in our power even when in the digital, without the pressure to come out of the broom closet or to share too much before we're ready.

For those who are ready for change, ready to embrace their weird and get their hands dirty with taking their magick and lives to the next level, *Unapologetically Magick* is the companion you have been waiting for.

INTRODUCTION

As I sit at my kitchen table and struggle to put down words, little thoughts jump in and out of my mind. I keep questioning myself and my abilities as an author, as a witch, and as an occultist. "Am I magick enough to write this?" I ask myself. Then more questions rush in, "What if people don't like the book or don't understand my beliefs?" And before long I have convinced myself that my voice is too small. This is perhaps the biggest reason I chose to write the book, because at some point it gets harder to shrink yourself down to size rather than embracing your magick.

This book is for the witches, the mystics, the seekers, the Pagans, the pantheists, believers, and everyone else who questions their path and where they fit but continues to learn and grow in their own understanding of what magick means to them. Throughout this book, I will talk about my own experiences and what I have come to believe or know based on my own understanding, but that is simply all it is: my own understanding. It is important that you read this book and only take what feels right to you, and once you have, apply those pieces to your own magick in a way that works. Don't try to fit anything into your life that doesn't genuinely feel like it belongs there.

This book with its title of *Unapologetically Magick* was called this because I still apologize a lot in my day-to-day life, and when I am in the zone with my magick, I feel most free and most myself. I'm not perfect; I question everything and change my mind an awful lot for someone who seems so stuck in their ways most of the time. I'd like to reserve my right to change my mind whenever I find information that teaches me something new or shows me that the way I was previously thinking about something doesn't really make all that much sense. The power to change our minds when presented with new information is special, and it also makes way for a less judgmental society at large because when we are free to change our minds, we allow others the freedom to do so without holding them hostage to their previous ideals. With that said, please know that my journey is still evolving.

Becoming unapologetically magick is about finding that part of yourself that knew all along that you had something special, that you had the power to set boundaries, that you could create your own life and it didn't have to measure up to anyone else's expectations. So much of my life up until a few years ago was full of people pleasing and making sure I was doing the "right thing" even when that thing didn't feel good or fit who I was inside.

There are a lot of people and things in the world today that will tell you how to act, how to behave, how to be you. It is an unfortunate truth that we live in a world where people are judged and condemned for their sexual orientation, gender, race, identity, and spiritual beliefs. It is important to listen to the voices of those who have been quieted. We must have the courage to do the right thing for others and for ourselves, and part of that is living our truth, whatever that may be. My truth, as it applies to this book and as I sit here writing now, is that I have, for the past several months, gone back and forth on my own belief system, working through religious guilt, my own queerness, and my identity as a witch.

If I'm going to be completely honest with you, as I think most writers attempting to write a book such as this should be, I've been struggling with being unapologetically myself in spaces where I fear being judged or misunderstood. All I can say for certain is that this book will not tell you what to believe or how to believe it. I will try my best to present an idea, and it is your right to either accept or reject that idea. This book will not tell you who you should be or what is right versus wrong; that isn't up to me to decide, and I'd have to be mighty high on my horse to think I could do so. This book is here for everyone who wants to be themselves in their spiritual practice without feeling bad about it. I hope that it offers a safe space to work through whatever needs tending to within your own spiritual practice and that it allows for a deeper connection with the Divine, however you know it to be.

Finally, being unapologetically magick does not mean that you need to be open in all areas of your life about the fact that you practice witchcraft or magick. There are many reasons why someone might want to keep their practice personal. This could be due to professional obligations, and although I don't like that there is still a stigma around witchcraft, I can't deny that at times it might hurt someone's professional career. Another reason might be because when something is personal, it could feel more sacred. Not everything is meant to be shared; that is a lesson I've learned the hard way over the years. It is okay to keep things to yourself, and witchcraft is an area that some people feel best about when they do. Either way, the choice is your own, and I hope this book helps you on your path.

SOME HOUSEKEEPING

Throughout the book, I capitalize the word *Divine*. I have done so because of my own belief that the Divine is in everything. I have more of a pantheistic view on things. Although that is my belief, it does not need to be your own. I do not hold the belief that there is one ultimate dogma, and my use of the capitalization is not to say definitively that there is only one god or creator.

Finally, throughout the book, I have included many journaling and writing prompts for you. There are many ways to go through these exercises, and I suggest tailoring them to fit you best. If writing is not for you, you may enjoy recording yourself on video or using an audio app. Everything in this book should be tailored to you because we are all different.

Chapter 1
WHAT IS MAGICK?

If you're going to be unapologetic about something it might be a good idea to know what it is first. The definition of magick that I'm going to share is one that feels right for me and has continued to feel right. It is important that you know you can come up with your own working definition for magick, as there are many paths and many ways of working it. Throughout my life, I came to realize that the world was a chaotic place and that much of it was largely out of my control. It is true that the world appears very chaotic and random, and that can be very overwhelming. This often leads people to try to control other things in order to feel better. There is also a phenomenon individuals experience within the chaos that is often referred to as *coincidence* or *synchronicity*. We will touch more on the topic of synchronicity in the second half of the next chapter, but it is a rather strange experience among the chaos.

The definition of magick that I like to use is that through the practical application of internal and external tools we can put ourselves in a position to have the chaos work for us to create certain predetermined moments of synchronicity. Through the acquiring of a magickal skill set we can mold the chaos. It could be really easy to just become afraid of the chaos and hide away, but if we can recognize that the chaos is neither positive nor negative—it simply *is*—we have a greater chance of aligning with it in a way that will produce results. The practical application of magick generally involves psychological elements, and although the success acquired through magick is sometimes referred to as the placebo effect or luck by those who are uneducated in our ways, what these prior definitions are often missing is the spiritual element of magick. Through the combination of practical, psychological, and spiritual elements, magick comes alive. Every witch, magician, and occultist should strive to put magick into practice and come to know its success for themselves. When you know and feel the success and healing of magick, it won't matter much what other people call it.

Another way of looking at magick is that it is a tool in achieving self-mastery. We are the microcosm of the greater macrocosm that is the outside world, meaning we are the rulers of our own small universe. This is not to promote having a god complex, but it is to say that you view the world through your own unique lens, and you have a number of things in your immediate orbit that you actually can control at any given time. Through achieving and unlocking the levels of consciousness that comes when we practice our magick and put to work our witchcraft, we can become masters of our own domain, and hopefully that will have a positive effect on the wider world. Throughout history, there have been many masters who reached the top of their chosen fields. Muhammad Ali made it to become one of the greatest boxing champions in the world. There are also many masters of writing and poetry, such as William Shakespeare, Toni Morrison, Maya Angelou, Sylvia Plath, Dylan Thomas, and so on. These people all worked hard to acquire the necessary skills to become masters. Magick is no different. It requires a level of commitment and focus to achieve mastery over the self. This isn't to say that mastery must equal a profession; it certainly does not. I personally believe it means to become the truest and most unique self, to embody the whole of who you are unapologetically.

In his book titled *Mastery*, Robert Greene talks about the true self versus the false self and shares an important message that rings true for the magickal path: "Your false self is the accumulation of all the voices you have internalized from other people—parents and friends who want you to conform to their ideas of what you should be like and what you should do, as well as societal pressures to adhere to certain values that can easily seduce you."[1] The path of self-mastery through the use of magickal tools allows you to peel back the layers of the false self and come to recognize the true self. The process is not always easy and can often be emotional as we grieve the self we once knew and fall in love with the truest version of ourselves. Greene goes on to say that it is a myth that only geniuses can achieve mastery or that it is only available to those born under good circumstances.[2] Mastery is available to everyone because it is a process of awakening to your self, the one that is free of the projects of others that have been placed upon you since birth. The true self doesn't speak to you in words but rather in symbols, dreams, and intuitive bursts. It will take time to develop the necessary skills and attune yourself to its language, but it can be done.

Similarly, in Devin Hunter's *The Witch's Book of Mysteries*, he writes, "The work of the student is to find the tools necessary to become the architect of their own lives. The work of the master is to be that architect, knowing every block, every trial faced, is a

---

1. Robert Greene, *Mastery* (New York: Penguin Books, 2013), 310.
2. Greene, *Mastery*, 310.

lesson from the very medium they sculpt, and that every triumph is a testament to the degree of intimacy they have with it."[3]

It is my hope to provide you with some of the tools that will assist you on your journey so that you will come to know that there is an architect and that power belongs to you. I will attempt to be as practical as possible in exploring ways that you can come to recognize the true self and live out the embodiment of your true self on a daily basis through the art of magick as unapologetically as possible. Witchcraft is as much about living life on your own terms as it is about the use of magick. To be free to be yourself is a very powerful thing.

WHO VALIDATES YOUR MAGICK?

Throughout this book, there is a central theme of coming to validate your own practice. Generally when talking about validation there is both external and internal validation. External validation is when an individual seeks approval and recognition from outside sources. This could look like approval from parents, friends, coworkers, or teachers. The risk of external validation comes when we change our behavior or take a different path solely because we don't want the people in our lives to disapprove. By doing this we risk drowning out the voice of the true self and never feeling fulfilled or living life on our own terms.

An example of this would be if you wanted to write books about magick but your parents disapproved, so instead of writing the books you stuffed the desire down and did something else, something more acceptable to them. This might make them happy, but it will rarely make you happy. What is really happening

---

3. Devin Hunter, *The Witch's Book of Mysteries* (Woodbury, MN: Llewellyn Publications, 2019), 8.

here is that the individuals in our lives project their own desires or ideals for their lives onto the people around them, and knowingly or unknowingly we internalize these projections and think they are our own.

This is why it can be a long process to recognize what are our own desires for our lives versus other peoples', because it has been happening to us since we were born. Similarly, we will be able to recognize moments when we, too, have projected our ideals onto other people. This often comes in the form of telling someone they *should* be doing this or they *should* be doing that. What is interesting about this concept is that if we can slow down and recognize when we are projecting our ideals onto others, we will come to see that we are often projecting our true selves without even knowing it.

In the digital world, external validation can also come in the form of likes and followers on social apps and platforms. This can turn into a toxic cycle if not addressed and one that we will speak about later in the book. If we are sharing our practice online, it might be best to do so out of a genuine desire to connect with others rather than to accumulate likes and followers. And if your practice only exists online and sways to the whims of online approval, it may be that you need to develop a personal practice offline that is grounded in your own validation first before choosing to share it. The digital space can be great for meeting other witches and magickal practitioners, but it can also be a tough place with a lot of misinformation too.

On the other hand, internal validation is approval that comes from within. It is an approval that needs no other form of validation. It comes from listening to the intuitive nudges of your true self. If the above example was reversed, and instead of choosing to not write the book you listened to yourself and wrote the book in spite of others' disapproval, then you would be going off of internal validation. In the end, you know what is right for you, even when making that decision can be challenging. Internal validation means that you will stick to what is true for you in magick and in the other areas of your life, and by doing so you don't betray the very nature of who you are.

The great paradox of life is that we are highly individual, yet we are also the same as everyone else. We are all a unique expression of the same energy. Coming to know your true self through magickal tools is allowing that unique expression to shine. The truth of the matter is that no one can tell you that you aren't magickal. You are deeply magickal by just simply existing. You do not need to seek the approval of others to practice magick or to walk the path of witchcraft.

Chapter 2
WAKING THE INNER CHILD

When we are younger, the voice of the true self is usually stronger. We aren't afraid to try new things and explore what sparks our interest. As we get older, this slowly changes as we are told what is expected of us at home and in society. I grew up in a controlling household, and it not only caused me to lose my own sense of identity, it made me begin to second guess myself at every turn. Part of peeling back the layers of the false self is coming back to the time when the voice of our true self was the strongest. For many of us, that is some point in our childhood.

When I was growing up, I thought that being an adult was going to be a lot of fun because I would finally be able to choose my own bedtime and eat whatever I wanted, and I wouldn't have to listen to anyone else but myself. I'm turning thirty this year, and I realized that the freedom I so longed for just got replaced with a lot of rules that were handed down to me by other adults and society's larger expectations for someone my age. What I thought was going to be all fun and games turned into a lot of stress, anxiety, and fear that I was somehow doing it all wrong. Early morning cartoons had been replaced with the news, and exciting trips to the mailbox were no longer treasure hunts—they were now just short walks that equaled receiving another bill. Today, there are chores and responsibilities to tend to, which leave no room for daydreaming or making wishes on dandelion fluff. We are told to "grow up" and to stop "messing around." We may fail to realize that magick doesn't just disappear because we stop believing in it. I began to realize that I had allowed myself to buy into the idea that I had to be serious all the time and that the things I enjoyed in my younger years were no longer important. I realized that a lot of what was lacking in my own life was harmony between being an adult and still caring for my inner child.

Life can be tough, but believing in magick and alchemy doesn't mean you are naive to life's hardships; on the contrary, often the people who believe the most have been through the toughest challenges. As adults there are constantly things that need our immediate attention and energy. We give focus to our careers, family, homes, and hobbies. So much of our life in our later years becomes so serious that we neglect the most straightforward way in which spirit speaks to us: through our intuition. Trusting in this inner voice is almost always the first act of rebellion against the "seriousness" we are bombarded with. Returning to sacred solidarity with spirit opens the door for magick to flow in and out of our lives as easily as the wind passes through city streets.

When awakening to the lost and forgotten inner child, we can put down our shields and relieve ourselves of the armor we wear to protect us from "silly thinking." And when we must do the serious work and take care of our responsibilities, we are also taking care of the child within. We can see harmony in being both the adult and the eternal child. Embracing the balance of grounded maturity and wisdom with a bit of whimsy gives the freedom to see and experience the full landscape that life has to offer.

When one first begins to become curious about magick, it may come on as a slow-burning curiosity and then, in most cases, it will bubble over to encompass everything. Many of the most straitlaced adults find themselves talking to their house plants and choosing tea blends to fit the day. A cloudy day often calls for a big, glorious cup of Earl Grey after all. These small gestures are little touches of magick that bring joy and offer the chance to enchant the mundane. Those who continue to explore this curiosity often find that the magick they believed in as a child has not disappeared but evolved into something very potent, highly powerful, and quite malleable. It is my hope that you never become so disenchanted by life that you stop believing in magick and that you can create a path that is all your own. When you customize your path, you are working directly with your true self to ensure that it is meeting your needs.

One of the ways that I first tried alchemy in my own life was by turning the chaos that was the way I spent my time into a structured schedule. By seeing that what I thought was freedom was actually restricting me, I was able to begin to find a routine that assisted rather than hindered me. My morning used to be a fight against the clock that somehow always resulted in a coffee-stained shirt and my forgotten lunch sitting on the kitchen table.

A few years ago, I was working a job that required long hours for little pay and came with a less-than-appreciative boss, who was more than happy to tell her employees that they were replaceable. I knew I needed to make a change. It wasn't until a string of bad luck and declining mental health that I finally summoned the courage to do my own thing. I started to read tarot part-time and began to really enjoy the level of freedom that came with it. For the first time in a long time, I felt alive and curious about the world again. Being so passionate about the work I was doing was a dream come true, but even that came with its own lessons. Because I loved my work so much, I had no problem working from the moment I opened my eyes in the morning until the moment I closed them at night. My relationships, physical health, and spiritual practice all started to suffer, and soon I came to the realization that my life needed harmony to feel good. I had to set boundaries for myself and make time for the things I cared about.

This same lesson replayed itself when I changed careers again and found myself spending hours upon hours online and aimlessly scrolling through social media. I loved the fact that I could work from home, but it also came with the challenge of setting my own schedule and keeping myself motivated to stay on task. I soon became tired of feeling like I was always losing time, and I decided to do something about it, which meant also making time for my spiritual practice and for doing daily activities that weren't attached to electronics.

A lot of things will require our attention every day, but if we can set a small amount of time aside for our spiritual practice and our magick, we will start to see the benefits at work in all parts of our life. Everything can be touched by magick, even your schedule or lack thereof. If you're reading this book, I'm guessing it is going to be important to you to make time for your magick and mysticism and to set boundaries, because no one else is going to do it for you, and everything is going to want a piece of your time. If you allow the energy of "take" to run your life, you'll have nothing left to give.

MAPPING OUT YOUR ADVENTURE

I know what you're thinking: creating a schedule is boring. But it doesn't have to be! Personally, I fought hard against creating a schedule and realized my inner child was rebelling at the thought of restraint. Instead, I began to think of it as mapping out my adventure so that, in the end, I could have more freedom. Mapping out your adventure may just bring you back to the energy of expansion and free you up to find your own unique path, and if it doesn't, that's okay too. In the end, this entire book is about finding what works for you, and there's no "one size fits all" here.

But before we move on to creating our map, it's important to quickly mention the magickal correspondences to the days of the week so we can use them to better create a plan for ourselves. It's easy to get stuck going through the motions from one day to the next and not realize how much energy one day can hold.

It should be noted that these are just guidelines and that if you feel strongly that a certain day has a certain energy, go with your own intuition, as this will lead to the best results for you. Here are the magickal days of the week and their correspondences:

Monday: Ruled by the Moon, this day can bring illumination and focus to tasks we have been avoiding and offer insight during times of meditation. Mondays are always multipurpose days for me, which means if I have a spell or ritual I've been wanting to do, instead of waiting until the end of the week, I can do it on Monday and start my week off right. Mondays are also great for focusing on anything health related, like workouts, meditation, and sleep to recharge. The Moon also rules psychic ability, so if you are wanting to work with your intuition or try some scrying, Mondays are perfect for divination. The Moon is associated with the color blue.

Tuesday: Ruled by Mars, this day is great for all kinds of physical activities and tasks that may cause exertion. Tuesdays are great days for putting an action plan together or getting inspired with new projects. This day may also be a time of confrontation, allowing you to confront relevant things, feelings, and thoughts with clarity. Mars is associated with the color red.

Wednesday: Ruled by Mercury, flowing from the motivation of Tuesday, you'll be able to organize your way to the top. Wednesdays are great days for decluttering, scheduling, and studying. It won't be uncommon to dive deeper into a book or start researching a certain topic that has been on your mind on this day. It is a day of balance, and because Mercury is connected to communication, you may find yourself writing, singing, talking, or generally communicating more on this day. Mercury is associated with the color yellow.

Thursday: Ruled by Jupiter, this is a day of creativity and greater spiritual connection. Thursdays can also be used for prosperity work. If you've been wanting to spellcast for something money related, Thursday is the day for it. Thursdays could also be great for gifting to your local charities or supporting small businesses in your area. Jupiter is associated with the color violet.

Friday: Ruled by Venus, this day is all about love, relationships, and romance. If you've been needing a date night or wanting to practice some love magick, Friday is the day to do it. It could be a day to treat yourself in the name of self-love or to meditate on the meaning of love from both a human and divine perspective. Venus is associated with the color green.

Saturday: Ruled by Saturn, this day is all about removing the blocks that keep us stuck. Saturday is also a great day for finishing projects, tying up loose ends, fixing up the house, or detoxing with a cup of fresh herbal tea. It is another great day for meditation and reflection that will allow you to go deeper into different and new ways of thinking or to see a fresh perspective on something you have been pondering. Saturn is associated with the color indigo.

Sunday: Ruled by the Sun, of course, this day is all about success, spirituality, restoration, and healing. Take time to greet the Sun during the day, whether that's by having your morning coffee outside or by getting out in nature. If you have been working hard toward a goal, Sunday is the day to visualize it coming together and feel the success of all your effort. Spend time in your spiritual practice today and rest when you need to. The week will start again, and this day allows you a moment of reflection before another magickal week. The Sun is associated with the color gold.

EXERCISE
CREATING YOUR MAP

Now you can begin mapping your adventures.

You will need:
- A calendar or planner
- Any craft items you like, such as colored pencils, markers, stickers, glue

The steps:

1. Get comfortable. If you have an altar space, you can light candles or burn incense, play some soft music, and call on the Divine to assist you.

2. When you are ready, perhaps with a warm cup of tea by your side, take out a piece of paper and make three columns. The first one is for the necessary things you *need* to do each week, like laundry, grocery shopping, cleaning the house, and taking the kids to dance practice. The second column is for things that you *should* do but aren't exactly necessary, like preparing lunches the night before, replying to emails at a designated time instead of 24-7, and scrubbing the toilet (no one loves doing this). The last column is for things that you *want* to do, like spend a day at the art museum, go thrifting for vintage items and cheap finds, or read a book outside under a tree just because.

3. Once you have your list, I'd like you to give it a careful look over. You may find a common theme happening. Everything serious and potentially boring is hiding in the necessary and should-do columns. Everything relaxing, fun, and potentially magickal is hanging out and having a party over in the want column. Why is this? Why have we bought into the idea that we must neglect all the things that bring us so much joy in favor of the household chores? What if I told you that *all* the columns are, in fact, necessary and that the most important part of this exercise is going to be harmony? Everything you

mentioned in the want column, everything that was just for you, is necessary for your spirit. These are the things that give your life energy and fuel. You cannot just shuffle your heart's desires off to the side and pretend to forget about them any longer. Little by little once you begin to incorporate moments of soul-nourishment into your days, you'll become more energized and freer, and you will be able to appreciate the moments of repetition while drying the dishes or pairing the socks out of the dryer.

4. The next step is to get colorful and creative and make a schedule that will be firm yet flexible when it needs to be, something that you can stick to and allows for the mundane and the magickal to come together. Practicality is the key here. If you're not a morning person and never have been a morning person, then I don't suggest making a schedule that suddenly has you up and out of bed at five a.m. You want this to be something that will stick and have you seeing magickal results. You don't need to get very technical with it; it can be as easy as Mondays are for solo coffee dates and devouring vintage books. At least once a week, take an hour or two for something that you find completely magickal. Let go of the notion that it must make sense to anyone else. Yes, it is important to think of others, but not at the expense of our own self.

5. Color your schedule, add different designs or pictures, collage over the edges—make it as artistic as you wish, and get off-the-wall creative with it. Step into the feeling of putting color to the page and

allowing the days of the week to pop out at you. Use the magick of each day and the planet it is ruled by to choose the best adventure. Nothing is too big or too small to be a part of this magickal disco of the free spirit and the responsible adult. Trips to the library or silently listening to an audiobook, making your own spell candles or divining with the tarot on a Monday night. The deliberate nature of this exercise tells the universe that you are ready and you are listening.

It is important to remember that you don't have to be perfect, and you may have to fight through the perfectionist hiding within. You are human—the universe knows it, you know it, I know it, your mom knows it … you don't need to be perfect or create a perfect schedule for this exercise to be effective. Try mapping out one week to start; this will allow you to make any necessary adjustments.

The act of deliberately planning some events in your week allows you to take the time to be conscious of how you are spending your time and how you could tweak the schedule to bring more balance and joy into your life.

Once you feel good with what you have mapped out for yourself, sit with it for a few moments, imbibing it with your energy. You can place your hands over it and visualize your favorite color electrified with light surrounding the pages. You can bless the edges with moon water or spell oil, again infusing your intentions into the movements as you do this. Place crystals at all four corners or in the center overnight, or place the schedule on your altar for further blessing and consecration. Take a moment to admire all the time and effort you've put into your work. Then, it is time to do a bit of grounding.

* * *

EXERCISE
GROUNDING

A grounding exercise is something that can complete a ritual by pulling everything together, blending the physical and the astral, allowing you to stay in that liminal space where you recognize that mind, body, and spirit are all connected. *Invoking* is a term used to describe calling on a deity or spirit and feeling its energy within you. The element of earth can also be invoked and used to bring a calming, centering, and nurturing effect.

You will need:
- A comfortable place to be
- Quiet or soft music playing (optional)

The steps:
1. You have several options available to you when positioning yourself to invoke the energy of the earth element. I suggest choosing what feels most comfortable to you and keeping in mind that you'll want to feel the energy flowing through you and connecting to the core of the earth. You can stand with your feet firmly planted on the ground, sit in a comfortable seated position with your back straight and crown of your head toward the heavens, or lie flat on your back with your palms facing down toward the earth.

2. After you are in position, close your eyes and picture yourself being surrounded by a vibrant green light. Stay here for a moment as you watch the light around you grow larger and larger. When you feel ready, imagine a string of green light leaving your heart and extending all the way down to the core of the earth. If you are standing, imagine the string coming from your feet if that feels easier for you.

3. Take three deep breaths in and out. Relax your jaw and your shoulders. Stay here for as long as you like. You should feel rooted and calm.

4. I usually have a cup of tea after a delicious grounding meditation, as it just feels like the perfect time for a hot beverage. You might enjoy one too, or allow yourself to intuitively choose the next right action for you.

* * *

EXERCISE
BELIEVING IN YOUR MAGICK

You've mapped your adventure and you've felt the calm energy that the earth element provides, now what? To end this chapter, I'd like to take you on another little adventure, only this time you can relax into your chair and allow yourself to be transported into another time and space.

To live a magickal and alchemized life and work your magick your way, I think it's important to explore the magick that we take for granted daily. When we understand just how enchanted even the most seemingly mundane events are, we begin to let the bigger aspects of magick into our lives. Before we dive into all the glitter, it's important to remember that not all parts of life are going to feel magickal and that this book is not about forcing yourself to be magickal 24-7. That alone feels like a nightmare, and as much as I do enjoy a dark myth every now and then, that is simply not what this is all about. I hope this book stands as a reminder that magick itself will not solve everything, but your spiritual practice can be the calm center of the storm. It can be your home and the place you go to when you need to work through the hard bits that life throws your way. It is for those moments, the ones that feel like a big cosmic joke, when you don't get the job offer or your relationship ends in heartbreak. It is at these times that we need magick the most. If you can't turn to your practice when you're in the thick of it, what is it even there for? In later chapters, we'll explore in more depth the concept of working your magick when you're in a wonky place, but for now, this is your reminder to include all parts of yourself in your practice, not just the positive but the parts that need it the most.

* * *

Jung and Synchronicity

Carl Jung, the late psychoanalyst, was an avid explorer of the concept of synchronicity, and it is this subject that I'd like to briefly discuss. The definition of synchronicity today is: the weird and often unexplainable way in which events that are unrelated by any cause or action appear to be related somehow. Jung had allowed himself to go into a state now known as "active imagination" in which he could indulge in the fantasies of his own mind and give free rein to his thoughts. This led to a series of precognitions about World War I. Ultimately, this had Jung asking questions like, what do synchronicities say about our universe? What does it all mean in the larger scheme of things? He felt that astrology could be deemed synchronistic in the way it housed the psychological archetypes and patterns that inhabit the collective unconscious. Many of Jung's theories are still discussed and utilized today, and in our own lives, many of us have encountered the mystery of synchronicity through seemingly unconnected events. The chances are high that at some point you yourself have heard the phrase "In the right place at the right time."

When we come to understand that synchronicity works with us and not against us, we can begin to bring magick into our lives and trust the flow of energy without needing to manipulate it or trying to change its direction. We can do as Carl Jung did with active imagination and allow our intuition to bring us from one place to the next, trusting that all things are coming together as they should. We can give ourselves the freedom to find practical solutions without becoming clouded by fear. Much of our life can be consumed by worry and self-doubt if we let it. Our magick stops being helpful because we aren't giving it the room it needs to work. When we recognize all forms of magick in our lives, we begin upon a great journey and find ourselves places we'd never expect!

Chaos Magick

Chaos magick is a form of magick that formed in England during the 1970s. One of the coolest things about chaos magick is that it consists of a set of techniques used to deliberately engineer synchronicity. In his book *Liber Null & Psychonaut*, Peter J. Carroll writes: "All magical paradigms partake of some form of action at a distance, be it distance in space or time or both ... In magic this is called synchronicity. A mental event, perception, or an act of will occurs at the same time (synchronously) as an event in the material world ... Of course, this can always be excused as coincidence, but most magicians would be quite content with being able to arrange coincidences."[4]

Anyone can begin to create and take notice of the synchronicities in their own lives and understand that magick is working in the background. How do we incorporate such practices into our busy modern lives? How do we fit magick into the day between folding laundry and cooking dinner? Mapping out your adventure was the first step in potentially creating more time for yourself and inviting magick back into your life. The next step is to become conscious and aware of the way it works in your everyday life. The more you become aware of it, the more you will learn to work with it. You don't have to be a seasoned chaos magician to use the benefits of synchronicity; all you have to do is allow where you put your energy throughout the day to work for your benefit.

Let's say you are working through a challenging project for work and you want to make sure your boss will like the result. You may think that the only thing you can do is to put effort into the project and hope for the best. I do agree that time and effort on the actual meat and potatoes is going to be important, but utilizing all the tools at your disposal, even if they seem unrelated, will bring greater rewards. Doing things like decluttering your home to bring a better flow of energy, enchanting your pens to bring the right words, eating dark chocolate to spark creativity, lighting a candle for good fortune, and telling another coworker that they're doing a great job are all things you can do simultaneously that

---

4. Peter J. Carroll, *Liber Null & Psychonaut* (San Francisco, CA: Weiser Books, 1987), 191–92.

will work together to bring about your desired result. Just like a good sports team uses all its players to their advantage, you, too, can use all the physical, mental, and spiritual resources available to you. In the above scenario, the individual not only worked on themselves and their project in an internal way, but also made steps externally to bring about change.

To round out this chapter, I'd like to add that the idea of believing in magick is not childish at all. Sometimes we might hide our magickal selves out of the fear that others might think we are simply fooling around. While I don't deny fooling around is part of the fun, I've had far too many experiences and successful results to believe magick is truly just make believe. Having a childlike love for magick is different than it being childish. If the past few years of exploring the ceremonial side of magick has taught me anything, it's that there is a group of people that take the education and practice of magick very seriously. The deeper I have explored and committed myself, the more I understand how powerful and transformative magick really is. It has taken me from a place of fear, self-doubt, and hiding in the comfort of my home, to feeling empowered and adventurous again. I don't claim to know everything, and as a matter of fact, I am reminded continually that the way forward is to remain humble.

Life can sometimes be like an old fairy tale, one that leaves you wondering whether the main character is going to make it out of the woods unscathed. Sometimes we find ourselves alone in the dark, standing amongst the tall swaying trees of our own forest. Sometimes we come across the wolves of our own story, and it isn't easy to tell their true intentions. Sometimes we just need a little time to gather our thoughts and find our direction again. A common theme throughout these tales is that the main character is often surprisingly unaware of their own power. If only in the beginning they knew how strong and capable they truly were, perhaps they wouldn't find themselves running from wolves or hiding from an angry evil queen. It isn't until they find and learn to use this power that the story takes a positive turn and they're able to stand up against the forces that have been haunting them.

Believing in magick, regardless of how big or small, is much like the kiss of life gifted by the one true love. I believe that this is because when you believe in magick, you believe in yourself. This is not another self-help book where I tell you to only use the law of attraction and hope for the best. I understand that there are very real systems in place that are there to keep people down and oppressed. I understand that it will take social and societal change to remove said systems and restore balance to what is currently unjust. What I am asking of you is to not allow the hardships you face to be the place you call home. I'm asking you to not allow the thoughts and opinions of others to become how you feel about yourself, and to know the power that you hold as an individual. Because if everyone feels powerless, then there will never be a unified existence. A spiritual practice can be a useful tool when bringing about change for ourselves and for our communities. When we have a spiritual practice to take our troubles to and a heart that still beats with whimsy despite all the things that tell it not to, that is, my dear friend, when we can begin to change the world.

Chapter 3

YOUR PATH IS NOT FOR EVERYBODY

To me, being unapologetically magick means becoming unapologetic about our choice to explore the path of magick. Although there may be different systems of magick, our paths often remain very personal and unique to us. Seeing as the path of witchcraft is often one that people will be on for a lifetime, there needs to be room for change, growth, and even U-turns. We must allow our path to change with us over time. Because witchcraft and certain forms of magick are so personal, our path might not look the same as others', and this is okay. When I first ventured into the world of online witchcraft, meeting people in the community and learning about their practices, I found two things to be true: The first is that, generally, people are kind, open, and willing to talk about the generalities of the Craft. The second is that not everyone is going to like you or the way you practice, and at the end of the day, they don't have to.

I began my journey many years ago through different books on witchcraft and tarot. I then moved to watching videos online of other witches talking about their paths. Over the past two years, I started taking an educational track where I was given a mentor. I felt like I wanted to see behind the veil. I wanted to know the mysteries for myself and see if magick really did exist. What I have found has been more than I hoped for. I have made friends, learned many lessons, stumbled a few times, and have come to a clearer understanding of who and what I am in the process. In *The Egyptian Book of the Dead* it says, "Behold thy soul is a star living."[5] I have come to believe the truth in this statement as an honoring of the divine and cosmic elements that live within all of us. I have found a love deeper than any love I have known previously, a love for the path I walk as a magician and witch, and for the divinity that lives within me. When I have thought about turning away, I have dreamed the symbols of the tarot, and they always seem to draw me back. Although I sought out a path that has a constructed method of learning, that does not mean I can't make it my own. Every part of your path will be unique to you. It is you that must go through the motions, put in the work, and ultimately reap the rewards of experience. Go forward unapologetic about your decision to do so. Begin and continue in confidence and share with others only what you feel you want to. In certain practices there will be a tradition of silence. Some things will be kept secret and given to those who are ready.

You don't have to share your practice with anyone; what you share and how you share is your decision to make. Each time we share something about our personal practice with someone else, we are taking a bit of a risk. We are vulnerable, and unfortunately, this can be taken advantage of. Not everyone is going to agree with your practice or even like it, and this is true for those who are in the witchcraft community and outside of it.

---

5. E. A. Wallis Budge, trans., *The Egyptian Book of the Dead: (The Papyrus of Ani) Egyptian Text Transliteration and Translation* (Garden City, NY: Dover Publications, 2020), lxvi.

This opens the door to discussion about unverified personal gnosis (UPG), other people's opinions, practicing in the open or in secret, and finding a way to balance between our own judgment and the outside consensus. All these things will come to matter to us on the path at different times and in different ways. Every time I think I have learned the lesson in seeing things in a more balanced way, I am confronted with another part of myself that only wants to see one side of the whole equation. We will always be growing, changing, and evolving, and part of the journey is about giving ourselves the grace to change and not being too harsh on our past selves for not yet understanding the whole picture.

UNVERIFIED PERSONAL GNOSIS

Unverified personal gnosis is when an occultist or magician comes to an understanding of something within themselves, a knowing, but this knowledge has not been verified by other occultists' experiences or cross-referenced in any way. We can see that consensus around different subjects within occultism has come to be the standard, and for the most part, this consensus is what people come to learn first as they venture onto the path. For example, when practicing color magick, it is generally considered a good idea to stick to the already-formulated correspondences that exist. These correspondences could be seen as verified gnosis, a consensus, or a generally agreed–upon truth. This usually looks like using the color red for love, green for money, orange for creativity, etc. These days, if you say you're doing a love spell and you use the red candle, you probably won't get much pushback on your decision of color. This same general consensus can be found in a lot of other parts of the path as we venture further into the tarot cards, crystals, or ways of spellcasting.

Unverified personal gnosis can at times look a little bit like going against the grain. If you sit with yourself and decide that love to you doesn't feel red, it feels blue, and you know this to be true for *you*, then using the blue candle is an unverified knowing but a knowing nonetheless. In a way, it could be argued that everything started as an unverified knowledge and it is only through people trying different things, talking about them, and sharing their findings that anything can come to be verified. In this way, we see that unverified personal gnosis and verified gnosis are quite similar.

If we only stick to the careful safety of verified gnosis in our practice, then we will only always know where others have gone, and we will only ever be doing what has already been done. Yes, there is a reason for verified gnosis, of course, such as when it comes to working with herbs. If it is known that an herb is poisonous, then of course you wouldn't use it in your practice in a way that would be harmful to yourself or others. Research is certainly important! You must know what a tool is and what it does before you can begin to wield it. In other words, you must know the rules if you're going to break them.

Will you explore the unknown? Will you allow your magick to mold the chaos? Will you explore the void? I've asked several questions, but they are all equally important, and only you truly know the answer that exists within you. There have been many magicians who have created their own spells, conducted their own carefully crafted rituals, and found something new. Many good books have been formed from such an exploration. Many good journals have been filled to the brim with such adventure.

Finally, you must consider whether you care about what others think of your own magickal practice. What if love *did* feel blue to you but everyone kept screaming, "Can't you see? Love is *red*!

Red! *Red*!" Will you break down and go against your own truth? Will you bend to their cries and set down the blue candle?

PRACTICING IN SECRET

In the modern age, there is much to consider when a magician sets out on the path, certainly far more to consider than first comes to mind. One of these considerations is whether to practice in the open, sharing with the world the fact that you are indeed a practitioner of magick, or keeping it a secret, perhaps only to be shared with a select few. This is not an easy decision to make, for each decision is an entire forest of its own with many sprouting trees. One should never do something at the peril of their own self; if it is not safe for you to practice in the open and this should cause harm to you in any way, then I suggest leaving it until you are safe to do so. It is okay to set magick aside and come back at a later date.

Let's focus on the choice to practice in secret. It is no less than the choice to practice in the open; in fact, it has its advantages, as often silence and seclusion can be quite illuminating. It may be easy to begin to think that those who are openly sharing their practices know more than you do, but that is not always the case. Perhaps you may fear that your practice won't matter if you are not sharing it, but is sharing it really such a necessity? Who else is more important than yourself? Who else has more to gain from your practice than you? If your practice helps you, then whether it is private or open will not matter much, for it will touch the lives of those around you regardless. You matter, therefore your practice matters. There are many methods that one can do in a private magickal practice that require no tools and will leave no clues to what you have been up to.

MEDITATION

Meditation, as with most things, is easier said than done, and it won't be for everyone. As for my own personal experience, I started to notice that my attention span was short. I felt like I couldn't concentrate on things for a long time, and I worried that having limited concentration would begin to affect my magickal practice. I noticed that when I meditated in the evenings before bed, I not only slept better but my mind felt at ease throughout the next day. Because of this and the other benefits that meditation has brought into my life, it is one of the practices I have kept up. Although, if you don't want to meditate and the act of meditation is something that immediately turns you off, you don't have to do it at all. Everything I am presenting to you is a personal choice; though, if you do choose to do it, there are many ways of meditating, and one may speak to you. Types of meditation include:

Sitting: Meditation by means of sitting still with your back upright (if you can) and your eyes closed can be beneficial; I have found that not trying to empty the mind but noticing when something comes into it and following it to see where it leads has worked for me. You may prefer to begin by setting a timer. It doesn't have to be long; you can try for one minute or five minutes. Keeping a journal with you could prove to be worthwhile, as you can record any significant thoughts, realizations, or symbols that come to you. These may all be significant to you upon further reflection.

Focusing on an Object: Still another form of meditation is focusing on a specific object, such as the flame of a candle. Concentrating on the light dancing, with its nature both beautiful and destructive, can bring to the surface a lot of knowledge that has been hiding within. Another object that can cause much occult knowledge to fill the mind is the tarot. Tarot is a tool used for both divination and occult exploration that holds all the possibilities of the universe. That's good news! That means by meditating on the cards and coming to understand the symbols and images for yourself, you can awaken to hidden mysteries and become even more successful as a magician, however success is defined for you.

Two Sample Meditations

Tarot is an excellent tool for self-exploration, and diving deeply into the symbolism is a chance to explore what's happening internally and externally. Often your true self will speak to you in symbols. It will appear in dreams, intuitive flashes, images in the mind's eye. Tarot is a tool full of symbols that can assist you in coming to understand how your inner self is speaking to you. Tarot is a tool of all possibilities, and even the smallest meditation on the symbols can produce profound results and realizations.

EXERCISE
TAROT MEDITATION

This is a simple, one-card tarot meditation, but the simplicity of it does not mean there isn't great knowledge to be gained. Often after meditating on a tarot card, I will record my dreams for the next week. Usually I can find some wisdom coming through about the nature of the card that is attached to the symbols in my dreams.

You will need:

- A tarot deck (If you cannot have a tarot deck, you can pull up the images of the tarot on any device. You can look through the cards and choose the one you feel most called to.)
- A journal and pen (optional) (You could also record with another device or practice the art of nonattachment by not recording at all. But, for further exploration of what may come to you in terms of meanings or symbols, it is usually best to record some of your own thoughts and reflections.)

The steps:

1. To begin, try to create an atmosphere that will be conducive to focus. This may look different for everyone. Personally, I enjoy the silence and being undisturbed while I meditate on the tarot. Another person might like to play classical music. You will know best what feels right to you.

2. Shuffle the cards, cut the deck into three, and then put the deck back together into one pile. Pull the card on the top and flip it over to reveal the image.

3. Do not pull over any other cards; this is a one-card meditation. One card holds an entire world of information.

4. Take the time to sit with this card. Focusing your gaze, drawing your eyes over each part of the card. You may notice that one part of the card immediately jumps out at you; ask yourself what this image means to you. Continue to look and you will find

that other parts of the card slowly make themselves known. Meditating for a few moments on what is coming to you as you look at the card will prove to be a worthwhile exercise.

5. Sometimes I find it best after I have meditated to cross-reference the symbols in certain cards with the symbols and reflections found in other books, such as Aleister Crowley's *The Book of Thoth* or E. A. Wallis Budge's *The Egyptian Book of the Dead*. However, if you are practicing in secret and cannot risk buying the books, that is fine. Tarot is a universal tool, and you will still get the information you are meant to receive.

6. If you choose to include a journal, you can begin to write down anything that comes into your mind—any words or images that come from those brief flashes of intuition. These writings may be useful to return to and reflect on later.

7. Finally, think of the tarot as a tool of great alchemy, as it has the power to take a stack of cards and imprint great wisdom into one's own mind. Once you have finished meditating on the card, thank yourself for giving you the time to do that! There will always be a part of ourselves that wants to do something else with our time, and by choosing to study or meditate on the tarot, you have overcome a part of yourself that might want to keep you stuck!

* * *

EXERCISE
TWO FOOLS MEDITATION

This second tarot meditation is one that I find fascinating because every time I do it, something new comes up for me. I hope you enjoy how simple it is yet how much knowledge can come bubbling up from inside.

You will need:

- The Fool card and the World card from the major arcana (You can also find the images online and pull them up on a device.)
- A journal and a pen (optional)
- A symbol of the ouroboros (This should be easily found online. It is the symbol of a snake eating its own tail and is often referred to as a symbol meaning infinity.)

The steps:

1. Begin again in an environment that is comfortable in order to focus your energy on the two cards along with the symbol of the ouroboros.

2. When you are ready, place the Fool card and the World card side by side. You may mentally think of the symbol of the ouroboros as you look upon the cards.

3. If you have chosen to have a journal, write down what thoughts, symbols, colors, and even feelings come to you as you meditate. I cannot say what will personally come up for you, but I can say that it will be significant and that, if documented, you will have the chance to return to it in order to gain further insights.

You can do this exercise for five minutes, ten minutes, or however long you like. Sometimes it is good to take a break and return to the same meditation again and again.

* * *

PRAYER

Prayer is also a powerful tool for connecting with the Divine and coming to one's own knowledge of the power they hold within. It is free, readily available, and requires no other tools than the self. Prayer is potent and perhaps a little underestimated in how quickly it can offer results when one is looking to gain some solid information. It is, of course, also a devotional act that can be tailored to fit that which you are praying to.

In her book *The Witch's Path*, author Thorn Mooney talks about the word *devotion*: "The word *devotion* comes from Latin via Old French and means to dedicate with a vow, to sacrifice oneself, or to consecrate something or someone, especially in the service of a deity."[6] She also talks about how the word devotion can feel too close to the word *worship* and is often associated with paths that witches don't feel comfortable on. Whether you see prayer as a tool for connecting with the higher self or the Divine, or as a tool for grounding, it is a tool that could help you if you choose to use it.

Prayer can happen in silent moments, while listening to music, or while singing a song. It can be with knees to the ground and hands clasped together, but it can also be so much more than that. It can be poetry written as a sacred act, it can be stirred into your meals as you utter a prayer over the food that you cook, it can be

---

6. Thorn Mooney, *The Witch's Path: Advancing Your Craft at Every Level* (Woodbury, MN: Llewellyn Publications, 2021), 60.

moments alone in the morning while you take a shower. Prayer does not have to have one face; it has many.

DEITIES

I am a firm believer that you do not need to reveal who or what you pray to just because someone asks for that information. Just like the decision to share photos of your altar, you also have a decision to make when you enter the world of open practice about whether or not you are going to get in the ring and start talking about your deity work. There also may be some magicians who don't believe in deity work, choosing only to work with archetypes. They may believe that they themselves are the god they work with and so they don't choose to work with an outside entity.

What deities another practitioner works with is none of my business, and to think it is, is an overstep of my own ego. When we venture into the world of open occultism, courageously telling the world who and what we are, there does come a choice of whether to share information about our own practice or keep it to ourselves. Whatever choice you make, also know that if you do share your deities, you don't need to explain yourself. Many people might ask why you believe in a certain deity. Let them ask their questions; it will be your own choice whether you choose to answer them or not.

CANDLES

Candles can be a welcome addition to any magickal practice, and when one must practice in secret, they usually won't draw too much attention. They are great tools for meditation when focusing on the flame. What is wonderful about candles is that you could have any color and still do all the magick in the world.

Usually, they can be found to be inexpensive, but of course you will always find more expensive versions, and so which type of candle(s) to purchase is a personal choice. When choosing a candle for meditation, I personally don't focus on the color; I find it easiest to set an intention for my meditation and then focus on the flame as it flickers. There will be times when my mind wanders and others when it is perfectly blank. What stays the same is that the flame is always there until the end.

READING NON-OCCULT BOOKS

Another way to practice in secret is to read non-occult books. This may seem contradictory to the mission to learn more about occultism and magick, but learning more about the world around you will teach you more about the world that is within you. It will allow you to become a master of your inner world, which in return could help the outer world. The macrocosm is vast and expansive; it holds all within it and is a reflection of the microcosm that is within us. Alternatively, the microcosm that is us is a reflection of the universe. I see this depicted within the universe tarot card, also known as the World. A woman rests in the balance holding two wands; around her wraps a snake that has become whole. By getting out of the microcosm that is occult books and reading books about the wider macrocosm, we can learn a lot about the occult and how to master our own universe.

This method is perfect for anyone who needs to practice in secret because you won't have a bunch of books about occultism lying around at the risk of being found, and you'll come off as looking rather intelligent with all your books that have their dog-eared pages filling your room. For example, I have learned a lot about myself in books about astronomy, psychology, philosophy, and personal development. Some of my favorite books for looking at my own behavior and my own projections are those written by Robert Greene. He does an excellent job of taking you through the stories of people throughout history and explaining their behavior while challenging your way of thinking. Others are those of Carl Jung; I find *The Red Book* to be a fascinating account of one man's exploration into the depths of the subconscious mind. I have also found learning about the cosmos to be quite exhilarating, as much of what we see happening today in the skies is also happening internally, often on a psychological level. Yes, that can be debated, but I find the cosmos to be a tool that offers great depth in understanding oneself. One book I particularly like is Dinah L. Moché's *Astronomy: A Self-Teaching Guide*.

SHARING YOUR PRACTICE

The methods as listed above for practicing in private are short, and there are other ways to practice in a way that will not draw attention to you. The methods mentioned are ones that I use quite often and that have proven to be more valuable than most of the group practices I have been a part of. I am a true believer that we have the knowledge that we seek already within us, it's just a matter of awakening to it and then allowing ourselves to believe the knowledge coming through us.

As for practicing in a more open way or presenting yourself to the world as a practitioner of magick, there are also some things to consider. Most of these considerations boil down to how much you are willing to share with others about your own sacred practice, about your own findings, and about your own understanding of the world around you or the connection you have to the Divine or gods. Coming out as an occultist, magician, or witch can be beneficial for finding community and having other people to speak with about different occult topics. It is important to be able to hear varying opinions and other points of view. It should also be mentioned that there are many people who are a part of magickal circles and orders that have not officially come out as a practicing occultist or witch. You don't have to out yourself in order to be a part of a community, and many established orders will enforce this rule by making it known that you should never reveal the names of the other members.

If you choose to share about your magickal path, you may be met with some resistance. There will always be people who think they have a say in what you should or shouldn't be doing. When we put our personal practices out there for the world to see, we put ourselves at risk of being judged and criticized. People will have opinions no matter what—sometimes that's all they have! It will always be up to your own comfort level what you choose to share and what you choose to keep to yourself. Here are a few things that people often debate about sharing openly, especially as we converse more in the online world.

Altars

There has long been the debate of whether to show your altar to the public via photos or videos, or whether to always keep your altar private. I have found myself on both sides over the course and development of my own practice. I have talked to practitioners on either end and found validity in both of their arguments. One of the first arguments I heard against sharing your altar is that if you are openly taking photos of the spells you are doing and sharing them with others, you risk opening the work up to outside energies that may want to sabotage your magick.

I have always thought of this as an interesting side to the debate, as I do personally believe in different energies and wanting to keep a spell contained and uncontaminated so as to allow it to carry out its original purpose, but I also think that if someone wanted to mess with us, they could try regardless. These days we share so much of ourselves through photos, videos, writing, artwork, etc. that if someone *really* wanted to try to cast upon us a spell of sabotage, they might already have a lot to work with.

Then, of course, there is the argument that the altar should be a sacred place for one to connect with the Divine, to share their most intimate selves, and to commune with infinite intelligences. The thought here is that because the altar is so personal in nature, it should be kept private, as it would be a privilege for someone to look upon it. Increasingly, I am leaning toward this argument myself, but I wouldn't tell another what to do with their own sacred space.

Alternatively, I have met practitioners who openly share their altars and don't seem to be bothered by it in the slightest. This could be a way to connect with others or from a desire to be more intimate and share their own world with the larger outside world. The choice here will always be your own to make. If you have an altar and you want to share it, then do so. If you don't want to share it with the wider world, then you don't have to.

Gnosis

This is a debate I often see, which ties into the Unverified Personal Gnosis section in the beginning of the chapter, and it usually ends with someone saying you should keep your own UPG to yourself. Again, I believe this to be a personal choice. The problem arises when we come to a conclusion in our own practice or feel we have gained some kind of knowledge and then we start to think that everyone must know, think, feel, or behave the same way as us about this thing. It can be quite off-putting when someone preaches to us about a part of our own practice.

When it comes to gnosis, which is a knowing or knowledge we have acquired on our path, we have a choice on whether or not we want to share this knowledge with the outside world. The same dilemma happens: if we choose to share our own findings, we open them up to judgment and criticism. If you know something to be true for you in your own practice, then anyone else's opinion really shouldn't hold that much stock. What I mean by this is, let's say you had what you would call an astral experience. You traveled out of your body, and you were surrounded by what you can only describe as a cloudy blue matter, almost like astral water all around you. Now, let's also propose that you feel like sharing that with the wider occult community. There may be some people who find it compelling and want to hear more, there may be some people who have had the same experience as you, and there may be others who think you couldn't have possibly had such an experience and will criticize you for sharing it. Sometimes we will have to weigh our own hearts and see if it will be worth sharing what we know. Alternatively, there have been many magicians who have come to know something and have had trouble putting it into words. Much of our experiences are just that: experiences, and a difficulty arises when trying to communicate those experiences in the form of human language. The astral world doesn't usually communicate with words; it communicates with dreams, symbols, and colors. Putting a truly riveting experience into words almost cuts the importance of it in half.

YOUR PRACTICE, YOUR CHOICE

I've touched on many important areas of personal practice, and it is my hope that this chapter allows you to see that there are often multiple sides to one topic. When we begin to see in a more balanced way, I believe we become more compassionate, understanding, and balanced toward ourselves and others. When we are free to find the truth for ourselves, our practice has a stronger and more stable foundation. Your practice is yours, and it does not need to be anyone else's. To understand this is its own type of freedom and an important step in being unapologetically magick.

Chapter 4
EVERYDAY ALCHEMY

Alchemy, as explained by Manly P. Hall in his book *The Alchemist's Primer,* is "based primarily upon one concept, namely, that an element can be transformed into another element. In other words, it is possible to take various substances, by art, change them and by doing so accomplish any one of a number of symbolic or literal ends, one of which was the transmutation of base metals."[7]

What is interesting about alchemy is that it does not just apply to turning objects into gold, silver, or any other metal. Alchemy can happen throughout our lives in many ways, and it can especially happen internally as we learn to get clear on what we want and begin to focus our energy on a particular task or desire. In terms of magick, I often think of alchemy as turning our emotions into powerful spells that will work for us in this world, the astral world, and beyond. Many a good curse has been laid due to the alchemy of emotion.

In the seventeenth century, a circle within a square within a triangle, began to be used to represent the philosopher's stone. The philosopher's stone was proposed to be a substance that would

---

7. Manly. P. Hall, *An Alchemist's Primer: Fundamentals of Esoteric Transformation* (Los Angeles, CA: The Philosophical Research Society, 2011), 5.

allow any base metal to change into gold or silver. According to Catherine Breyer, squaring the circle can also hold philosophical and spiritual meaning. Squares are often seen as representing the physical world because of the number of things that appear in groups of four in nature: the seasons, directions, the classical elements, to name a few.[8]

One of Leonardo da Vinci's most famous drawings is the Vitruvian Man. It depicts a man with two sets of arms and legs enclosed in a circle. Within the circle there is a square, although the edges of the square spill over and extend outside the bounds of the circle. The general theme of the piece is that the earth, the Divine, and the human are all connected. In this we can see that humans are inherently one with the all and one with the earth. If what is infinite cannot be destroyed or undone, it cannot be less than, and if it is added to, it becomes more of what it already is. Therefore, humans as a depiction of divinity must hold the all within. This is why many good astrologers will say, "Don't just listen to your Sun sign, because we have the entire solar system within us; we have the cosmos at our fingertips." I have heard this said about the tarot cards as well: if the tarot is a tool that holds all universal possibilities and humans are a container of the universe—a microcosmic depiction—then we must have all tarot cards within us. When I look at da Vinci's Vitruvian Man, I think about how whatever happens in the microcosm also happens in the macrocosm, thus the magick we do internally can echo forth out into the wider world. Alchemy, when used to perform magick and change our circumstances, starts from within.

---

8. Catherine Beyer, "What Does Squaring the Circle Mean?" Learn Religions, Dotdash Meredith, updated January 16, 2019, https://www.learnreligions.com/squaring-the-circle-96039.

The Hermetic arts follow something known as the "wisdom of the whole universe," and it is often characterized by the combination of astrology, alchemy, and magic—gifts that were said to be handed down by the Greek god Hermes. Blending the three specialties together creates something new all on its own; it is indeed a form of art. It is my hope for every occultist, magician, and witch who opens the pages of this book that they can create their own form of art, mixing their own occult specialties and coming to know their truest most potent power and nature. Let's look at some of the forms of everyday alchemy.

EMOTIONAL ALCHEMY

Emotional alchemy is what happens when we use our emotions to change our environment and to work our magick. Emotions are a very important part of magick, and the more deeply that we feel them and connect with them, the more powerful our magick can be. I have found it easiest to become attuned to the energy you are wanting to work with; for example, when casting a love spell or casting a spell for prosperity, the practitioner must be filled with emotions of love, happiness, joy, and openness to receiving.

I have heard it said that emotions are like guideposts that show us important things throughout our lives and can point to things we have even kept hidden from ourselves. Take jealousy, for example: it is often seen as a negative emotion and one that we shouldn't have. Jealousy can be a great tool, one that we shouldn't cast aside so quickly. By becoming aware of our emotions, we can begin to see them for what they really are and for what they are trying to tell us about ourselves; this level of understanding will also help us come to know our truest paths and aid us in our magick. Usually when I am jealous of something, it is because I want something that another person, place, or thing has, *but* unless I explore the feeling of jealousy deeper, I never get down to what is *really* making me jealous. There are times when I see artists creating and making a full living from their art. Their lives, from what I can tell across a screen, look full of adventure and passion. Sometimes seeing artists making a living from what they love gets me a bit jealous. One might think, it's because you want to be an artist yourself! This may be true to some extent, but usually if I explore my jealousy deeper, what I really want is their level of freedom.

This same thing can happen when feelings of sadness, anger, frustration, guilt, lust, worry, happiness, joy, or disappointment come up. I have noticed in my own life that when I have a strong initial emotion, if I take the time to explore it, I can usually find something more concrete under the surface. When I want to explore an emotion to alchemize it and use it in my magick, I usually start by journaling about it and creating a list. If you don't enjoy journaling, you could do this exercise in other ways such as speaking it out loud, recording it on a voice app, or creating a graphic to represent your emotional process. With any of these methods, you can do this exercise as often as a strong emotion comes up, and it will allow you to see what goes on underneath along with other possible contributing factors including moon phase, day, weather, location, time, and ritual activities. We will be discussing magickal record keeping deeper in a future chapter.

Types of Spells and Their Emotional Correspondences
Let's first explore different emotions that line up with different kinds of spells. This can be a helpful guide, but it is not a full guide, nor is it going to always be accurate for your own personal use. Be sure to take the time to think about the spell you are casting, the desired outcome, the length of time in which you want the outcome to happen, and how each emotion can assist with all of this.

Love Spells: These spells can range from bringing new love, enhancing existing love, making one desirable, and assisting with self-love. Emotions for these spells will include but not be limited to love, passion, lust, desire, courage, curiosity, happiness, and the feelings associated with being open to new experiences.

Parting Spells: These spells can be performed to break a certain couple apart, to separate yourself from a loved one or ex lover, or to separate yourself from a certain situation, job, boss, project, etc. Emotions for breakup spells will include but not be limited to anger, guilt, sadness, happiness, frustration, and feelings associated with freedom and well-being when looking to the outcome of the spell.

Prosperity Spells: These spells can be performed when one wants to enhance their finances, bring new opportunities, find a better career, get a boss on your side, find networking opportunities, generate a new circle of friends, and more. Emotions for prosperity spells will include but not be limited to happiness, joy, love, desire, openness and welcoming, gratitude, courage and grit, and feelings associated with success and abundance.

Luck Spells: These spells can be performed to bring about good fortune, turn a streak of bad luck around, help one to feel more confident, and open doors of opportunity. Emotions for luck spells will include but not be limited to happiness, joy, elation, confidence, courage, self-love, empowerment, feeling lucky, and feelings associated with the universe being on your side.

Reversals: These spells can be performed when a practitioner has good reason to suspect someone is working magick on them. This can happen if another practitioner is jealous of you, sends you ill will, or wants to harm you in some way. Reversals return that energy right back to the sender. Emotions for reversal spells will include but not be limited to anger, affronted, courage, strength of spirit, empowerment, and frustration.

Banishing: These spells can be performed when a practitioner wants to remove an unwanted energy from their personal life, home, or work environment. Banishing spells can be performed on people, negative energy or spirits, situations, habits, or any other thing that one would want to quickly remove. Emotions for banishing spells will include but not be limited to courage, feelings of freedom, empowerment, strength for boundary setting, and feelings associated with feeling calm when thinking of the desired outcome.

Hexes: These types of spells are usually performed when wrongdoing has taken place. If a practitioner feels wronged and has enough justification or needs to magickally put someone in their place, a hex can be used. A hex has a shorter lifespan than a curse and will do the trick to get someone to stop bothering you. Emotions associated with a hex could include but will not be limited to anger, ferocity, disgust, pity, fear (if you want to instill it into the other person), rage, disappointment, courage, sometimes heartbreak, and other feelings associated with being wronged.

Curses: These types of spells are usually performed when one has been wronged and when the practitioner wants to prolong a spell in order to bring about more change. Or they can be used to really hit home the point that you shouldn't mess with certain people. A curse has a longer lifespan and can be carried over generations. Emotions associated with a curse are similar to that of a hex but may be more intense, and the spell itself will be conducted and carried out over a longer period of time. Feelings like anger, rage, disgust, vengeance, horror, fear, worry, disappointment, and other feelings associated with being wronged will work for a curse.

Psychic Enhancement: These types of spells are performed to bring someone better understanding of or clearer communication with their psychic abilities. They can be for clearer dream symbolism, more focus, and enhanced claircognizance, clairaudience, clairvoyance, clairgustance, clairsalience, clairtangency, and clairsentience. Emotions associated with psychic enhancement will include but not be limited to curiosity, openness, calmness, gratitude, focus, happiness, and feelings associated with enlightened senses.

Glamour: These types of spells are performed in order to change one's appearance, attract a desired form of attention, help someone to keep a disguise, or enhance one's self-love. Emotions associated with glamour spells will include but not be limited to love, self-confidence, esteem, passion, happiness, mysteriousness, and courage.

The emotions associated with each spell will need to be more specific and tailored to the individual spell itself. For example, if you wanted to conduct a spell to help you study, you would need to first feel the emotions of studying, such as focus, calm, stable energy, and desire to learn. Then, you could move through to feeling the emotions of passing the test that you are studying for, which might be happiness, joy, excitement, and relief.

A Note about Hexing While Angry

Before we move any further with this chapter, it is important to speak about spellcasting while experiencing negative emotions. First, it is okay to cast spells while angry, frustrated, or hurt. Magick is a way to take back our personal power, and sometimes all we have is that magick. That being said, the spells we cast are powerful, and when done correctly, they work. Casting a spell in the form of a hex should match the reason for the hex. What I mean is, the punishment should fit the crime. Before casting a hex, make sure that you have thought it through; if you need to, take some time and make sure that you really want to cast the hex. Spells like this take time, energy, and effort—often over a period of days. Do you really want to spend all that time hexing someone? All that energy to cast the spell? All the effort and willpower? If, after you have thought it through, you decide the person is indeed wrong and deserves the hex, then proceed. Still, there are a few other things to consider.

If you are still in the early stages of anger, you must consider if the type of hex you are casting is an overreaction. Not an easy thing to admit or think about during that time, but it is necessary. For example, if someone has cost you your position at work, is it fitting to cast a hex that will take away their career, home, *and* marriage? That might be a lot. Instead, it might be more fitting to cast a hex that will have them start coming to work late, forgetting important appointments, being unable to focus, and ultimately getting fired. Before you cast a spell with such emotions, do your due diligence and make sure that you cleanse yourself and keep up your own personal protection work.

Now, with that out of the way, we can use the journal exercise mentioned above to tap into our root emotion. This will aid in achieving powerful results, and offering our emotions to our spellwork is one of the best ways to ensure a spell will work, especially those that will need more time to come to fruition.

EXERCISE

**TAPPING INTO YOUR
EMOTIONS FOR SPELLWORK**

It is my guess that if you find yourself wanting to cast a spell you will already have the emotion you are feeling readily available, but it is important to focus that emotion if you want to actually see an outcome. For this reason, I think tapping into your emotions and getting clear on what it is you are feeling before casting the spell is important. The more potent, the better.

You will need:

- A journal and pen

The steps:

1. Begin by thinking back to a time when you felt a strong emotion, particularly one that lines up with a spell you want to perform. This could have been on your birthday, during a movie, while using social media. There will have been a time when something

came up that made you feel some sort of way, and this is what we are going to use to go deep and see the concrete underneath the dirt.

2. Write the emotion you felt (sad, mad, jealous, happy, etc.) at the top of the page. Underneath that, write down the situation that made you feel that way.

3. Next, take some time to create a list of all the reasons you can think of as to why that emotion came up for you at that point in time and in that exact situation. This may seem easy at first, and you may jump to write down why you felt a certain way; of course the answer is obvious! Don't stop there, take the time to peel back the layers.

4. Once you have indeed peeled back the layers, you may begin to see some connections. For example, if my upbringing was full of turbulence, never having a solid foundation, my own fear of success, which is really a fear of change, could be rooted there. This would leave me to understand that my fear of success might be more managed by feeling secure where I am and taking small steps to reassure myself that I will be safe when things inevitably change. Take some time to find the root of the emotion.

This exercise is particularly helpful when casting spells that directly align with that emotion. Once you have finished, you can use the confirmed emotion and true reason in your spellwork. This can also be used to create a sigil and practice sigil magick.

* * *

Alchemizing Your Emotions

By now, you should have a spell in mind and have uncovered the very heart of your emotions, and now it is time to alchemize them! For demonstrative purposes, let's decide to cast a spell for good luck. Let's say I've been having some bad luck in terms of missed appointments and missed opportunities. Now, this is an interesting phenomenon that can also happen when someone has a hex placed upon them. In Jason Miller's book, he describes the symptoms of an external attack, saying, "This often starts by a mild feeling of being out of step with time, as if you can no longer manage to be in the right place at the right time … This can be accompanied by patterns of bad luck, and of everything you touch going wrong."[9] There have been times when I felt like my bad luck was due to something being sent my way, and I used some of the methods in Jason's book to send it back and then cleansed myself and my space using a combination of the Lesser Banishing Ritual of the Pentagram and some good old chaos magick that consisted of laughing out loud in every room of my house.

For the purposes of moving forward, let's say I have ruled out anyone hexing me, and I feel confident that I have just run into my own string of bad luck that I would like to turn around. The first step in any spellcasting of this nature is to feel empowered and confident enough in your own abilities. Of course, if you are wavering on that front, it's okay; I've been there. At times like that, you can lean on the magick. I always say, if you don't yet believe in yourself, you can believe in the magick; that will see you through. Now, if I'm suffering from bad luck, I may already be feeling a bit worried or fearful of what could happen next, which might

---

9. Jason Miller, *Protection & Reversal Magick: A Witch's Defense Manual* (Franklin Lakes, NJ: Career Press, 2006), 30.

fuel the next unfortunate situation that I encounter, with my own fears setting off a chain reaction of sorts. To ensure that I cast a proper spell for myself, I'll need to recognize what I'm feeling and begin to understand what emotion my good luck spell will require while I'm casting it.

EXERCISE
CLEARING THE ENERGY

The first step would be to recognize that I may have worry and fear surrounding my bad luck. In this case, I would spend a moment before casting the spell to cleanse myself. One way of doing this is to shoot the energy of worry and fear out and away from you.

You will need:

- For this exercise, you won't need any special tools, only yourself.

The steps:

1. Begin by standing or sitting in a position and place where you will be able to focus for about two to three minutes. (It is important to note that this exercise can also be completed entirely in one's own mind and any physical movements are merely suggestions.)

2. Think of the feelings and emotions you want to remove. This will be a temporary removal for the sake of conducting your spell. All emotions are temporary, both when we feel them and when we don't.

3. Now picture a light (any color that you feel connects with banishing; I often gravitate toward an electric

blue) and feel this light begin to surround your entire being. Feel it surround your physical body, your inner being, and your etheric body.

4. Once you have been covered in light, begin to push your arms out in each direction: north, south, east, and west. As you do this, exhale a large breath, and say, "Shoo, [fear]; you have no place here." After you have pushed your hands out and felt the energy of fear leave in one direction, clap your hands together to signal that the energy cannot return.

5. Stay a moment in the light you have created, and when you are ready, move on to calling forth the emotions you *do* need for the spell you have chosen.

* * *

EXERCISE
CALLING FORTH EMOTIONS

The previous exercise is one you can do before any spell you conduct. Often, practitioners will prepare their space and their body, mind, and spirit before performing a spell or ritual. This can be by way of bathing and physically cleansing beforehand, prayer and reflection, calling upon divine sources, and cleansing a space, such as an altar or working room. How one comes to perform the spells they choose will look different, but one thing remains true: each practitioner holds power, and no one can take that away from them.

After you have cleared any emotion that doesn't belong in the spell, you can begin to conduct your good luck spell.

You want to turn your luck around, and so you will first need to think of the emotions you want to feel when you are experiencing good luck. I imagine that I might feel pretty good, happy, content, confident, and like I am walking on a cloud. These are the emotions I want to fill myself up with when going into the good luck spell. After I have covered myself in an electric blue light, I would then call forth all the emotions listed. I sometimes find it helpful to attribute colors to different emotions.

You will need:
- For this exercise, you won't need any special tools, only yourself.

The steps:
1. Standing or sitting in a comfortable position, begin to think of a rainbow full of beautiful colors—each color representing a different emotion, one that you would like to call forth for the purposes of a spell, in this case good luck.

2. Next, imagine the colors coming at you from all directions and connecting to you. They fill your hands, your arms, your chest, your stomach, your legs, your feet, your neck, your head. They begin to extend beyond the physical body and out past it. They begin to fill your etheric body, and all around you is a kaleidoscope rainbow of color and emotion.

3. You can now say out loud or in your mind, "I am happy, I am confident, I am content, I have good luck, I feel as though I am walking on a cloud, and fortune has smiled upon me."

4. Once you feel ready, you can move on to the spell you have chosen to conduct.

* * *

EXERCISE

GOOD LUCK TALISMAN

Now it is time to conduct the good luck spell. This spell is one that I have created and performed a few times when I wanted to boost my luck and success rate for obtaining opportunities. In this case, I like to charge a magickal talisman and keep it with me. Some talismans are let go of after their purpose has been achieved, but I see a talisman for good luck as something that you can recharge as needed and keep with you over a long period of time. It may assist you with a plethora of situations, such as during a job interview, opening your eyes to see new opportunities, being in the right place at the right time, or when starting a project. A talisman for good luck has always felt like a good idea to me.

You will need:
- A coin (any kind that you feel a connection to)
- Incense (jasmine, sandalwood, myrrh, or cinnamon), you could also use a cinnamon stick
- Salt
- A bowl of water
- A candle (any color your feel connects with good luck like green, orange, etc., or use the agreed-upon consensus of white for all purposes)
- Lighter or matches
- A nail or other carving tool to inscribe the candle

The steps:

1. Begin by creating a space to conduct your spell. You will be lighting the candle, burning incense, and combining elements through these tools, so choose a space that can get a little messy for a moment. If you have a working altar, you can perform the spell and talisman charging there.

2. Focus your intention on good luck and all the emotions that come along with it that you called in previously. When your workstation feels covered by the energy of good luck, begin with the next steps.

3. Inscribe the candle with the words "good luck" or "good fortune." While doing this, continue to set the intention and bleed the emotions into the work.

4. Light the candle in the center of the workstation. Beside the candle, place the bowl of water and the incense.

5. In front of the candle, place the coin and begin to say a spell you have prepared for good luck. Preparing your own words always feels the best, but if you don't have any, here's something I usually say: "May this coin be filled with the energy of luck and fortune, may it bring the one who keeps it great prosperity and confidence, may it bless the one who holds it and be the key to unlocking that which they desire most."

6. Next, light the incense and pass the coin through the smoke, saying, "May the winds of change bring good luck my way."

7. Pass the coin through the fire and say, "May the heat of flame remove all blockages to luck."

8. Place the coin in the bowl of water and say, "May the strength and fluidity of water bring luck down every channel of my life."

9. Take the coin out of the water and place it in front of the candle again. Now sprinkle salt upon it and say, "May the salt of the earth ground my good fortune and make it long lasting and prosperous."

10. Now hold the coin in your right hand, saying, "This coin is my good luck charm; it is here to assist me and bring me good fortune. When I hold it and when I think of it, I will be blessed with good luck."

11. Now hold the coin in your left hand and repeat again, "This coin is my good luck charm; it is here to assist me and bring me good fortune. When I hold it and when I think of it, I will be blessed with good luck."

12. Now place the coin on your heart, covered with both hands, and repeat for the third time, "This coin is my good luck charm; it is here to assist me and bring me good fortune. When I hold it and when I think of it, I will be blessed with good luck."

13. Place the coin back on your workstation and allow the candle to burn down. Once the candle has burned down, you can choose to keep the coin with you, carrying it in a bag or in your pocket, or you can keep the coin in a safe place either on your altar or another place. It will serve as a tool to use when you need a boost of good luck.

* * *

Because we've spent a considerable amount of time with the example of changing one's luck around, it is only right to mention that after a spell has been conducted, especially for such a change as luck, there is some maintenance and upkeep. There is a reason that magicians practice daily protection rituals. They cleanse their space and banish unwanted energies.

Sometimes spells don't stick because the practitioner reverts back to their old patterns and habits. For example, if someone conducted a spell to make their relationship better and for a while everything was going okay but then the original spellcaster started to fall back on old patterns, like not picking up after themselves or not spending quality time with their partner, chances are things would go back to the way they were, and the spell would look like it hadn't worked. Maintenance is just as important as the spellcasting itself. Often, if you can keep up the maintenance, your need for long and drawn-out spellcasting sessions will greatly diminish.

THE ALCHEMY OF IDEAS

Moving on from emotional alchemy, another thing that I strongly feel is alchemy is the ability to pull ideas from the universe and turn them into something material. I love the idea of imagination as magick, and when a practitioner can enter the stream of consciousness that allows for ideas to freely come forth, that is a beautiful experience. Often, we hear creative people saying they aren't exactly sure where they get their ideas from, they're just happy that they keep coming. It is also true that multiple people can have the same idea, because ideas are just small blips of inspiration. To turn an idea into reality takes hard work, motivation, and determination. There might be many obstacles in someone's way in the form of financial roadblocks, educational roadblocks, time roadblocks, or resource roadblocks. I have known many ideas to come and go in my own life, only to find them somewhere later, having become something through someone else. If we are honest with ourselves, I'm sure we have all experienced this. I don't believe that we have a shortage of ideas; I truly believe that we each have a shortage of time and energy, which only allows us to focus on a few ideas at a time. This means we must choose wisely.

How does one begin to alchemize ideas? The first step will be to pluck an idea out of the universe and decide that this idea is a worthwhile pursuit, one that would be suitable to bring into the material world. How do we spark the idea machine? Many creatives have found ways that work for them; I have heard of people working at the same spot and same time every day, believing that this routine will allow them to tap into the idea machine. I have heard of changing things up, having new scenery and new experiences as a way to spark inspiration. I've heard of people like George Washington Carver, a great scientist, going out into the woods and surrounding himself in nature to talk to God, who gave him ideas.[10] I've also heard of ideas coming to people through dreams and visions, and of course there are people who don't stress about it but just wait because they know the next idea will come their way.

These are all possible routes to take, my preference being in nature and having some resemblance of a routine that lets the universe know I am an open receiver. I am of the feeling that if we let the universe know that we are an open and willing conduit,

---

10. Iowa PBS, "George Washington Carver: An Uncommon Life," YouTube video, 56:04, May 8, 2018, https://www.youtube.com/watch?v=_3CVmluYFtI.

it will use us for the creation and manifestation of ideas, and they will be sent to us however we are to receive them. Many nights I have had a dream that I didn't understand at first, but I thought it significant enough to write down. Many times these dreams have been useful to me in the creation of something in the physical world. I have found that a simple prayer, almost like a short meditation, can do the trick to get into the state of mind that is needed to be open to receiving ideas. The biggest blockage to receiving these ideas is that we start to second-guess them. We begin to put labels on the ideas as they come into our mind, deeming them either good or bad. Then, we may start to worry about where the ideas are coming from, if they will keep coming, or if we are going to ruin it all and the ideas will somehow just stop. What *really* stops this flow of ideas is this process of labeling and worrying about the whole thing. If we can individually find a way to open ourselves up and stay open, then the ideas will come, and we will be able to choose for ourselves which ones we are best suited for.

EXERCISE
TAPPING INTO THE IDEA HIGHWAY

I have, on occasion, felt as though some ideas weren't right for me. It was as if they came rushing into my mind from the lightning highway above us solely because I was an open conduit and nothing more. It is okay if you feel like some ideas just don't fit; that's all part of the process. What matters is that you first get the ideas flowing, because you need the initial idea to alchemize it into something material. Here's a small meditation I do before I sit down to write or before I go for a walk, just a little something to get the ideas flowing.

You will need:
- An open mind

The steps:
1. Begin by relaxing the mind and body. This can be done through a gentle breathing exercise where you breathe in for the count of three and exhale slowly for the count of three. Repeat this as many times as needed until you feel calm and focused.
2. Place your palms on your legs facing up, or out in front of you facing up, if you can.
3. Say with a confident voice, "I am an open conduit ready to receive all the ideas the universe is willing to give me. I will be a scribe for all that I am given. I will align with the ideas that best suit me and allow the others to live on freely through others. I am a grateful alchemist ready to transform thoughts into reality."
4. Now, picture a highway of light running above you. Ideas zip from one end of the highway to the other. Take your fingers and begin to pluck ideas from the highway of light. These may not be real ideas right now, but you are telling your mind that you are ready.
5. Remember, you don't have to act on them all, but begin to document them. Over the day, carry with you a notepad or voice recorder, or use your phone to record ideas that you receive. Once you begin to be an open conduit, the universe will know where to send its information.

* * *

Once you've got a good list of ideas, preferably around some-thing you'd enjoy doing or setting into motion, take some time to think about which idea you want to start with. During this time, I like to "play the tape to the end" and really start to imagine what my idea will look like and how it will change the world when it comes to fruition. I go from the beginning of the idea and think about what the result will be. By fully imagining it, I believe there is a greater chance it will happen. Of course, this also means I must think about how much time, energy, and resources it will take to see my idea become a reality, but there is something magickal about understanding that you can bring something to the world and be a creator more than a consumer.

Different ideas will take different amounts of effort. Take this book for example—getting the idea for it didn't take much effort; it sort of just popped into my head one day and stayed there. After that, I spent time writing a book proposal. This was a bit more effort, as for a nonfiction proposal you must have the outline, an author bio, and a few sample chapters. Once a book is acquired, the author usually receives half of the payment for the book and the other half once they hand in the finished manuscript. This is where the real effort begins. Writing a book takes a lot of time, research, and days of sitting at the computer typing words onto the page. Once the first draft is finished, there are a series of edits that must be done, and once the publisher is happy with it, a cover is designed and the book is created, put onto shelves, and put up for sale on online stores. As you can see, one small idea starts a series of actions that affect more than the individual who had the idea, and just like that a chain reaction forms until there is a fin-ished and final physical product.

Bringing emotional alchemy together with the alchemy of ideas is something that works well. If you can think of the desired outcome, of how you will feel once your idea has become something in the world, you can use that emotion to create a spell that will help you bring your idea to life.

THE ALCHEMY OF SELF

A whole self-help industry has grown to assist people with becoming the best possible versions of themselves. This is an interesting concept, and I do enjoy self-analysis, but as I grow older, my idea of self-help has begun to change. I believe that we are always changing and evolving; the person I am at this exact moment is not the person I will be five minutes from now. Is there one ultimate, best version of myself? I don't think so; it is more fluid, and we operate on a spectrum most of the time.

However, self-analysis could help us to understand ourselves better, which could lead us to living in a way that aligns better with our core values, thus creating less friction as we move through the world. If we understand ourselves, we have a better chance of understanding the world around us and being kinder and more empathetic to other people. If we can understand the depths of our own being—the positive qualities, the more negative qualities, our own motivations and desires—then we will have a better understanding of the motivations of others, and perhaps this would lead us to being more patient when someone rubs us the wrong way. It almost gives us an insight into our own intentions and how our intentions lead to actions, and that allows us to see the underlying intentions in other people.

Some people view magick as more of a psychological model rather than a metaphysical one. The macrocosm exists within the microcosm and vice versa. What is interesting is that a lot of what we do in the magickal realm does have positive psychological applications, such as meditation, repetition, and being open minded. According to Sean Martin in his book *Alchemy & Alchemists*, "The Swiss psychologist Carl Jung believed that, whatever sort of gold the alchemists were looking for, they had in fact discovered the unconscious, and that their frequently strong, challenging images were portraits of various states of consciousness that could lead us into a greater understanding of ourselves."[11]

This could mean changing their physical health through getting better sleep, meditation, daily exercise, and generally taking care of themselves, but this change could also come from seemingly smaller changes that grow over time into something much larger. A person could change a small daily habit that starts another chain of events, allowing them to end up in a new place a year from that moment. They could also decide to change their schedule, start a new job, go to therapy, start a new hobby, or invest in free online education. All these small decisions allow a person to change their circumstances and potentially their path in life.

Depending on different magickal systems, an individual might find themselves using different tools in the process of self-analysis. Shadow work has become something of a buzz phrase throughout the spiritual community, but it does offer a chance to look at the parts of ourselves that we often leave hidden. The *shadow* is a term coined by Carl Jung, and in the book *Jung Lexicon: A Primer of Terms & Concepts* by Daryl Sharp, the shadow is described as the "hidden or unconscious aspects of oneself, both good and bad, which the ego has either repressed or never recognized."[12]

---

11. Sean Martin, *Alchemy and Alchemists* (Harpenden, UK: Oldcastle Books Group, 2015), 31.
12. Daryl Sharp, *Jung Lexicon: A Primer of Terms & Concepts* (Toronto: Inner City Books, 1991), 123.

This means that what we think is the shadow really isn't the shadow. It was only the shadow *before* we recognized it; once we have pulled it out of the depths and acknowledged this hidden part of ourselves, it is no longer a part of the shadow. The shadow being both good and bad is also subjective because what one person finds positive, another may not. The act of uncovering the unconscious part of ourselves is a very personal process, as no other person can definitively tell you what is or is not the shadow within yourself.

An example I love to use is that of being a repressed creative. If you grew up being told creativity didn't sell and you would be wasting your time trying to be an artist, you may have never explored the creative part of yourself, and it may remain there, hidden in the shadow of the unconscious mind. If you continue on through life always getting jealous every time you see a thriving artist making money from their work, this could be a serious emotional indicator that you have something hiding in the shadow. If you took the time to explore this, you may find that a part of you is very creative and longs to be able to express itself. There are many ways to begin shadow work, but the biggest suggestion that I can give is to just begin to be aware of the things that trigger strong emotions in you. Use the exercise from the section on emotional alchemy to go over the past thirty days: what made you happy, mad, angry, jealous, concerned, joyful, and excited? In each of those answers, there will be clues to what lies in the shadow, and there you will find another part of yourself.

Another interesting tool is that of the birth chart. Analyzing your own birth chart is an exercise I highly recommend, as it gives you time to think about which aspects you feel drawn to and which aspects you tend to avoid. It also allows the practitioner to digest how they feel about their overall chart and if they believe they can do anything about it. For example, upon analyzing my own birth chart, I noticed that I would struggle with maintaining meaningful relationships. This is something that has been true throughout my life, and seeing it confirmed in my birth chart made me feel a bit better about my social awkwardness. While I was writing about my birth chart, it dawned on me that I now knew something about myself and that just by having this knowledge, it meant that I could do something about it. What is most interesting about studying your own birth chart is that although we can follow the agreed-upon consensus for what different planets in different houses mean, along with the other more in-depth correspondences for astrological placements, the practitioner has the ability to deem a placement positive or negative for themselves. They may also see different things at different times in their lives when analyzing their own chart. I'm sure I would have found different placements more positive in my twenties than I do now in my thirties. Later on in the book, we will talk about the birth chart again through the eyes of a black hole metaphor, but for now it is interesting to think about the fact that we may be able to alchemize our own placements within our birth chart.

EXERCISE
ALCHEMIZING YOUR BIRTH CHART

To do this fully will take a considerable amount of time but would be beneficial. Each aspect of your birth chart tells you something about yourself, both from the consensus of meaning and from your own gnosis. This exercise will take you through analyzing and alchemizing one placement; it will be your own decision if you would like to take it further.

You will need:

- A copy of your birth chart (can be found online using a chart calculator)
- A journal or way to record your thoughts
- Access to placement meanings (You can look this up online or, for a deep dive, you can use *Llewellyn's Complete Book of Astrology.*)

The steps:

1. Start by taking a look at your chart and finding the Moon placement and noticing which house and sign it falls under. For example, someone could have their Moon in the ninth house and be a Taurus.

2. Next, spend some time looking at what this means both positively and negatively. For example, the ninth house is attributed to spirituality, religion, higher education, and philosophy. The ninth house is ruled by Jupiter and the sign of Sagittarius. Having a Moon in the ninth house could make someone very free-spirited, romantic and sexual, adventurous, materialistic, and good at keeping secrets.

3. Create a chart with two columns on a piece of paper, placing the things you like about your Moon sign in one and the things you dislike about your Moon sign in the other.

4. Once you have finished creating the chart, it is now time to analyze the columns. You may find that some of the characteristics are opposites of each other, or you may feel that each side is more or less neutral. Perhaps the book you are reading or the online

page you are pulling information from is giving you "good" qualities and "bad" qualities about your placement. It is us who can ultimately decide whether a placement is positive or negative in our own unique situations. Each characteristic has the ability to benefit you or harm you; it is all about balance.

5. If you feel strongly that you are pulled to one side or the other—for example, if your Moon sign has the tendency to have your head in the clouds daydreaming all the time and you think this has become a hindrance to you—then by recognizing this you have the ability to change it and balance out some of that energy. Many of the forces within your birth chart can work for you rather than against you once you come to understand them.

6. Continue to do this with each placement as you see necessary. Take your time; it is a process that happens over weeks, months, and years rather than something that happens in one day.

* * *

Now, we can move on to another fun tarot exercise centered around the same theme.

EXERCISE
TAROT WALK THROUGH

Finally, a powerful tool for exploring the self is the tarot. When flipping through the tarot initially, you may come to find that you gravitate toward some cards more than others. You may have cards that are your favorite or that you feel good about when they come up in a reading. You may also find the opposite—that there are certain cards you dislike and can't stand to see come up in a reading. This concept has always fascinated me because the cards that I love will not be the same cards that the next person loves. We will all gravitate to different cards for different reasons. This makes the tarot a very personal and explorative tool, one that is perfect for both shadow work and inner child work. Here is a very simple exercise that may allow you to find clues and doorways into your own shadow so that you may begin to alchemize the self.

You will need:
- A tarot deck
- A pen and paper or voice recorder (optional)

The steps:
1. Take some time to get comfortable and prepare yourself to sort through the tarot deck.
2. Decide whether you want to go through the whole tarot deck (seventy-eight cards) or just the major arcana (twenty-two cards).
3. Now, in a rapid-fire way, begin to sort the cards into two piles. The first pile is for cards you like, and the second pile is for cards you dislike.
4. Once the cards are sorted, now comes the time for some introspection and analysis. Start with the dislike pile. One by one, pick up the cards and ask yourself, "Why have you put this card in the dislike pile? What about it do you dislike? Where are

these feelings coming from?" This exercise may take some time, so if you need to focus on one card for an extended length of time, that is okay, and it is perfectly fine to step back and return to this exercise over the course of several hours or days.

5. When you are ready, move over to the cards you chose to place in the "like" pile. Analyze them, spend time flipping them over and looking at the illustrations. Think about the name of the card and what you feel it represents. Why do you like the card? What part of it speaks to you?

6. During this exercise you can journal about each card or document it in another way, such as through a voice recorder. Take note of when you discover something new about yourself or when a certain card takes you down a path of emotion or memory. You don't have to find something new right away, but over time you will start to see new patterns and new sides of yourself depicted in the tarot cards. Often while looking at the cards, I see new things in the illustrations that I had previously missed, which is always funny because I have been looking at the same tarot cards for years.

7. Take as much time as you need. When you are ready, give yourself some thanks for taking the time to explore yourself and your shadow on a deeper level.

* * *

Our spells and our magick will begin to align with our truest path, and we may find them working with more accuracy. Alchemy allows us to explore the world in relation to ourselves and design a path forward. The occult transformation is a beautiful thing! People begin on a path that often brings them out of hiding and into their true selves. I wish you all the best on such a transformative journey as this.

Chapter 5

TAROT ROYALTY

The tarot has been in my life for a long time, and over the years of reading for myself and others, I have found that different elements of the cards will jump out at you at different times. By meditating on the cards, shuffling them around, turning them upside down to see them from a new perspective, new information comes to the surface. The interesting part of it is that someone could look at the cards for years and still not know all that is held within.

For the sake of this chapter, I have chosen to stick with the symbolism of the Rider-Waite-Smith tarot deck. It is one of, if not the most, widely used tarot decks, and many of the modern tarot decks have based their symbolism upon the Rider-Waite-Smith. The deck was originally created by Pamela Colman Smith, who was the artist, and Arthur Edward Waite, who had commissioned the art for a tarot deck. Throughout the deck, there are many occult symbols and meanings, and as you continue to work with the tarot, you will uncover layers of information. The Rider-Waite-Smith deck has numerology, astrology, and ancient Egyptian symbols embedded into each card.

SELECTING A TAROT DECK

Selecting a tarot deck is one of the things that really brings me joy in life. We are in a time when there are so many options and so many creators who are passionate about the decks they make. When working with tarot, it is important that you are able to find a deck that speaks to you. Just like the path of witchcraft, when you find a tarot deck that resonates with you, it will be in your life for quite some time. When selecting a tarot deck, it is important to like the actual art and be able to pull something from it. Art is very subjective, and that's part of the fun. I personally like bright, bold colors and direct symbolism. The fun of exploring a new tarot deck is that in most cases you will be able to look at the artwork before purchasing.

Many decks these days also have a portion of the funds going toward different causes, and so that might be an important element to you when looking for a new tarot deck. Another is that of the guidebook. If a guidebook is important to you, then of course you will want to select a deck that is accompanied by a proper guidebook. I find that the guidebook is important if the art is more abstract, as it also reveals what the artist may have been thinking or may have been inspired by while creating.

I enjoy tarot art that is full of detail because when I read, I look for expressions on the face, body language in the cards, the scenery, and other symbols like animals. As you move into exploring more tarot decks, you might find that cardstock is a make-or-break element. Having a thin and flimsy cardstock is something I don't like because it makes shuffling a chore, and the cards don't last as long. Like any good friendship, when choosing a tarot deck you will just sort of know when one is right for you. Depending on where you're at in your tarot journey, you could also choose a different deck for different purposes. I know professional tarot readers who have one deck they keep for themselves and a number of different decks that they use when reading for others. Perhaps you want one deck that you will work with solely for your dreams, another for shadow work. Choosing a deck is personal, so take your time and don't be afraid to experiment and look around.

Finally, once you have made the choice, then you can get to know the tarot deck, which is also a very fun and illuminating process. Getting to know a tarot deck takes some time and can look different for everyone. There is something very sacred about just sitting down with a deck of cards and seeing what comes out of your own mind. It is quality time with yourself; it is an act of sovereignty in a small package. The best way I know how to get to know a deck is to use it, to flip through the imagery and to begin to put your own meanings to the cards. Think of situations in your own life that speak to the nature of each card. Through this process you will come to have a deeper connection, and your cards will be linked to you in memory and in the physical as you sort through them. Going beyond the guidebook is often the next necessary step when befriending a deck of cards.

THE ROYAL CARDS

Whenever I need a self-love boost, I consult the royal cards of the tarot and vibe with their energy. Each card represents a different aspect of oneself, thus making them a useful tool for exploring the way we think and feel about ourselves. Each suit also represents an element: wands (fire), pentacles (earth), swords (air), and cups (water). The royal cards offer a mirror, and every witch knows that mirrors are great for reflection work, glamour magick, and some forms of protection magick. The tarot is a tool for all of that and more.

Even the most put-together, self-loved human being on the planet has their moments of doubt and insecurity. The best thing you can do when you begin to doubt yourself is to say, "I feel you, I understand that you are fear in disguise, and I will not let you stop me today. I know my worth is nonnegotiable, and I choose to step forward." Sometimes you just need a reminder, and that is where the royal cards come in.

Let's look at each of the royal cards.

King of Cups

The element of this card is water. In the Rider-Waite-Smith illustration, the King sits upon a throne amidst a wave-filled sea with a boat in the distance and a fish jumping out of the water. He is dressed in elegant robes with a crown to match and a necklace with a fish hanging from it. The face of the King looks stern, and his eyes are looking forward across the sea. You can imagine him looking at the land; perhaps he is able to see quite far away to where the Queen of Cups sits.

This is a very interesting card when you break it down; to me it has always felt as if the King is a genius at spotting opportunities and seizing them. His gaze shows that he can see clearly where others cannot. Although the waves are all around him and the ship in the distance is rocking, he remains calm with confident body language.

The King of Cups is a reminder that when you start to doubt yourself or start to feel like you have drifted too far out to sea, you are still royalty. Sometimes we must drift a little in order to find the right part of shore. With all of the water, it can represent the emotions we feel as we go through life—our waters won't always be steady. Love yourself enough to be the calm for yourself and to accept opportunities when they are given. This card also offers a warning: love yourself enough to ask for help; you don't always need to be stranded in the middle of the sea.

Queen of Cups

The element of this card is also water. In the Rider-Waite-Smith illustration, the Queen sits upon the shore on her throne. She is dressed in a long robe and hooded cloak; a large golden crown sits upon her head. In her hands she holds a lidded cup with elaborate-looking handles. She looks down intensely at the cup, almost studying it; her eyebrows look furrowed. Where the King was amongst the rocky waves, she is steady and supported, resting nicely on land.

Emotionally this card can represent a calm and reserved approach. Perhaps the Queen has worked hard to understand her own emotions and knows how to handle them. Her conscious mind feels studious, able to focus on the task at hand. Subconsciously there may be more at play, depicted by the sea at her feet. The lid on the cup can signify that she has something important kept away and secured. It also may show that she is able to remain calm by bottling up her emotions and may lash out on occasion. There is always balance within the cards. The Queen of Cups is a reminder to take care of your emotional health. Even though we live in a world where we are supposed to be calm, cool, collected, and always put together, we need to have a form of release.

King of Swords

The element of this card is air. Air is representative of our minds, thought patterns, reasoning skills, and general intellect. In the Rider-Waite-Smith illustration, the King sits amongst a landscape looking larger than life, towering above the trees; two birds fly above the clouds. He is dressed in blue robes with a crown upon his head. In one hand he holds a sword, on the other he wears a ring. He stares confidently forward as if to look directly at you.

Behind the King on his throne are a number of butterflies, which feels like the end of a metamorphosis. The caterpillar has transformed and so has his way of thinking and seeing the world. With his head seated among the clouds, he is able to see long distances. His thoughts are both his freedom and his own prison.

The King of Swords reminds us that there is power in forward thinking and planning. Those who do not plan ahead may have a hard time navigating the terrain when it gets rough. Even if you enjoy going with the flow, there is a time for adapting and a time for strategizing. This card is a reminder of balance, as you can be too much in the mind and not enough in the body. Find ways to move when you feel stuck in your thoughts. When someone is always in their minds, they are often quiet and tucked away somewhere to think, or they are observing everything around them silently. There is power in being a quiet observer and gathering your thoughts until you are ready to speak.

Queen of Swords

This card is also an air element. In the Rider-Waite-Smith illustration, the Queen sits with her right side facing the reader; she is looking forward to the east, her left hand is raised, and the palm is open. Her right hand holds an upright sword. The crown on her head is made of butterflies, and her robes have images of clouds on the fabric. The sky at the top of the card is a clear blue with one lonely bird flying overhead; the bottom of the card shows a number of clouds, and she, too, sits atop her throne looking larger than life.

The crown of butterflies feels like the same kind of meaning from the King card: an evolution of thought process, an illuminated mind, as if having stepped over a threshold mentally. The way she is sitting makes me think of the stream of consciousness or the stream of thoughts. She is aligned with the flow of energy that brings ideas, and ideas breed opportunity. Meditation is what comes to mind when I see this card because with a good meditation practice you are able to focus your thoughts and can learn to empty your mind. Admittedly, anytime I think I have emptied my mind, I suddenly realize I've been caught in a daydream that went unnoticed for some time. Only on a few occasions thus far have I felt like I was truly able to hold on to a sliver of "oneness."

This card is a reminder that even if we think we have missed out on an idea because we didn't act soon enough, there will always be others. When we connect with the Divine or the energy of the universe, we will always be blessed with ideas and creativity. It is also a reminder that we can communicate clearly and speak up for ourselves and our boundaries when needed.

King of Wands

The element of this card is fire. In the Rider-Waite-Smith illustration, the King looks as if he is looking over his right shoulder; his face is turned slightly away from the reader. In his right hand he holds a wand. His robes are made of elegant colors: yellow, orange, and green. His throne looks as if it is made of gold and has symbols of lions and lizards; on the ground runs a lizard by his feet. The sky is a clear blue, and the land looks like a barren desert.

The King of Wands, although he may look stern and preoccupied, is a very charismatic character. He can bring people together for a common cause and create friendships with ease. The crown that sits on his head looks like golden flames, and the lizard on the throne behind him completes a circle with its tale in its mouth. There is an infinite cycle of action and reaction, death and rebirth, energy and renewal.

The King of Wands is an action card. It reminds us to go after our desires and be present in our lives. When the King of Wands has an idea, he puts it into action and through that action sees the results firsthand. Many times, we may sit idle waiting for things to come to us; even when we cast a spell, we must put work into producing the outcome. Even magick takes work, action, and energy. This card is also a reminder that for everything we are only mediocre at in life, we have a few things that we are great at. Whether something has just come naturally, or we had to work for our mastery, we have the potential to hone our skills and become leaders in a chosen field or niche. We don't have to take that to extremes either. If you want to be a leader in the tech space, go for it—you will rock it. But if you are the one that can cook awesome meals at home for your family, that means just as much. The King of Wands is a reminder that you are royal at something, and don't ever forget it!

Queen of Wands

The element of this card is also fire. In the Rider-Waite-Smith illustration, the Queen sits atop a golden throne with images of lions on the back. Atop her head sits a crown of gold; in her right hand she holds a wand, in her left a sunflower. There is a black cat sitting at the base of the throne looking directly in the reader's direction. The Queen herself looks over her left shoulder as if to look over at the King. The sky behind her is a clear blue, and there are some mountains in the distance.

The Queen herself is strong like the lions that sit on either side of her throne. Her intuition is on point, and she knows how to use her magick. The way she is seated with her back straight and posture wide, gives us the impression that she is confident and sure in who she is. The sunflower in her hand has fully bloomed and so has the love she has for herself. The sky being so clear on both of the wands cards gives the feeling that any obstacles can be overcome; the strength of these cards is enormous.

King of Pentacles

The element of this card is earth. In the Rider-Waite-Smith illustration, the King of Pentacles sits atop a throne with two bulls; he is surrounded by plants and vines. In his right hand he holds a staff; in his left he holds a large coin. Behind him in the distance is a castle, and the sky is clear. He looks down at the coin in his hand to study and admire it. He has amassed a great wealth, and he is able to enjoy it so long as he does not become too arrogant in his riches.

The King is grounded, loyal, and sometimes stubborn. There is an energy of protection and a feeling of being able to fight if provoked. With the castle in the distance, there is the symbol of material wealth and possessions, yet he is sitting away from it. The plants that surround him point to a knowledge of how to multiply wealth and nurture his finances. He has spent a long time learning not only the art of business but of money itself.

This card is a reminder that even though much of our lives is spent with work, there must be balance. Our work cannot sustain our entire lives; there is meaning in every part, and it is not wise to neglect family, friends, and home life for too long. To be too focused on and obsessed with money is not a goal that anyone should have. If you only focus on money, you miss out on real relationships and the meaning behind doing something with purpose rather than solely for profit.

The Queen of Pentacles

The element of this card is earth. In the Rider-Waite-Smith illustration, the Queen is seated on her throne with images of goats on the sides. All around her there are flowers and vines; in her hands she holds a large coin. Her head is tilted down toward the coin, and her gaze is resting softly upon it. In the distance there are blue mountains and, on the bottom right of the card, there is a bunny that almost blends in with the land, so you must look carefully.

The Queen is nurturing of her environment and knows how to tend well to the plants and animals that are around her. The mountains in the distance may signify that she has had quite the journey but has found a place of solitude and success. She is able to care for herself, and by doing so, able to care for others. Her body language looks as though she is tucked away and distracted, lost in her own thoughts.

This card is a reminder that we may need better time management and that a shift in schedule may be needed. It is a loving reminder that we cannot do all things in one day; reaching our goals takes time and patience. We can nurture our ideas and watch them grow, but it won't happen overnight. It can be really easy to get discouraged these days when it seems like people are able to get successful and achieve their dreams with the snap of a finger. We must remember that everyone's path is different and that behind most successes there are trials and errors.

EXERCISE
ROYALTY RITUAL

The Kings and Queens of the tarot offer you a chance to explore the fullness of being human while remembering that you are worthy of greatness. They don't dismiss the struggles that we face, but they don't allow us to forget who we are within our struggles either. When it comes to self-love and self-care, one of the things that I have been doing is a royalty ritual. I spend an hour surrounded by the Kings and Queens of the tarot, quiet my mind, and allow myself the time needed to bless myself and hear the messages that are coming to me. Our lives are so busy with work, school, relationships, hobbies, and chores. An hour of time in ritual is a priceless getaway.

You will need:
- Tarot deck
- Four small white tealight candles
- Jasmine incense (can substitute for another kind if needed)
- Lighter or matches
- Journal and pen
- Music (I like calming meditative music, but the choice is yours.)
- Pillow or folded blanket (something comfortable to sit on)

The steps:
1. Take all the King and Queen cards out of the tarot deck and pair them together—King of Swords with the Queen of Swords and so on.

2. Next, you will create a cross with the tarot cards; you can also think of it as creating a circle.

3. Take the King and Queen of Swords and place them facing north.

4. Take the King and Queen of Pentacles and place them facing east.

5. Take the King and Queen of Wands and place them facing south.

6. Take the King and Queen of Cups and place them facing west.

7. Next, place one tealight candle beside each of the tarot card pairs.

8. In the space in the middle of the cards, place your pillow or blanket and take a seat. Get comfortable. Slowly breathe in and out. Feel your shoulders release tension, your arms and legs soften.

9. Now take a moment to think about your intention. It might be easiest to set the intention of focusing on the self. Allow whatever messages of self-care and self-love to come through as they need to.

10. Once your intention is set, light the candles starting with the swords cards, then pentacles, then wands, and finally cups.

11. Light your incense and consecrate the space with the smell of jasmine.

12. Now is the time when you can play soft music, or you can sit quietly and allow thoughts to come to you. Gaze softly at the cards and try not to judge your thoughts as they enter your mind, simply allow them

to be. You can also use the remaining tarot cards by shuffling them and pulling a few. They may serve as a starting point for thoughts and messages.

13. As the messages come to you, write them down in your journal.

14. The messages may feel as if they are coming from the Divine or from the universe. You might also feel like it is your own intuition talking to you. If you choose to, you can record the messages you receive from each card in your journal. This is something I personally enjoy doing, as it gives me the chance to return to the messages at a later date to see if anything else comes up.

15. Spend as much time here as you need to. When you are ready, blow out the candles one by one. Thank the Divine, the universe, or yourself for being there. Put the tarot cards all back together into one deck, and one last time light the incense and bless the space with the smell of jasmine. I hope that you received some lovely and nurturing messages, just the kind you needed.

* * *

DAILY AFFIRMATIONS

Another way to use the Kings and Queens is with daily affirmations, especially when you need a good royal boost. You can create affirmations with any tarot card, but for the purposes of this chapter we're going to stick with the royals. You can use these affirmations the same way you would any other. Write them down in a journal or on a piece of paper that you can carry with you. Text them to yourself or record them on a voice memo to save on your phone. Write them on sticky notes and stick them to the bathroom mirror. Place them wherever they are going to help you the most.

These are the affirmations that I use. I suggest that you create your own because they will be so much more powerful the more connected to them you feel. However, if these resonate with you, feel free to use them.

King of Cups

"I will have compassion for myself, especially when it is hard to do so. I will give myself the same compassion that I give to others. I will forgive myself for the mistakes I have made and for who I was before I knew better. I will not burden myself with the weight of perfection. I will embrace the freedom that comes with being human."

Queen of Cups

"My intuition knows what I need, and it guides me with ease. I will trust in myself. I am both the calm and the storm, the ship and the water. May I know my worth, and may I never turn away an opportunity just because I don't feel worthy. I am strong. I am capable. I am Divine."

King of Swords

"May I know that true strength comes not from hostility but from gentleness. May I remember my own faults before I judge another. May I be kind but uphold my boundaries. May I know the power of my words and use them wisely."

Queen of Swords

"I am my own protector. I have the power to stand up for myself. May I respect myself and do what is needed even when it's tough.

May I stand up for what is right even when it is hard. May I always return to my own true north, and may I recognize the voice of my true self as it speaks from within."

King of Wands

"I am creative because I am Divine energy. My creativity is my birthright. May I use it to its fullest while I am here. May I not hold back out of fear or self-doubt. May my art reach the people it needs. May my inner child be expressed and my creative self be nourished."

Queen of Wands

"May I be the kind of friend I wish to have. May I hold the hand of someone in need and may mine be held also. May I listen without needing to speak and be heard when I speak. May I love myself through all of life's phases and understand that I will change in cycles just like the moon."

King of Pentacles

"May I come to understand what true abundance is. May I be open to receiving and opening my pathways to what I need and deserve. May I lead always with my heart and with service. May my service be what brings my life nourishment."

Queen of Pentacles

"May I understand that life needs death, that the flowers need rain, that love needs loss. May I feel worthy of accepting the gifts that each offers me. May I always be able to connect with the Divine force when I feel lost and unsure. May the flowers bloom wherever I grow them from the kindness bestowed upon them."

ROYALS IN THE SHADOW

The royal cards can also show us our shadows. Because they are each connected to an element—earth, air, water, and fire—they are also connected to those parts of our lives. We hear all the time that life needs balance, but rarely do we dissect what that means or what we need to do in order to have that balance and maintain it. Royals can help you focus on why you might not feel "royal" or worthy, and you can work backward to find the solution.

Sometimes, though, you won't easily find the answer, and it is important to remember that just understanding is enough. Oftentimes I have journaled my feelings over a tarot card and found no conclusions until a week later while doing some mundane tasks. Suddenly the answer comes to me, and I can see how to move forward. I used to try to force the answers out of the tarot and in the process made myself very frustrated.

A prime example of this is when I would shuffle the tarot deck and ask a yes or no question, something like "Will I become a full-time tarot reader?" Then each time I pulled a card, it would come back with the corresponding answer for that card: "maybe." You see, there are certain cards in the tarot deck that are not a "yes" or a "no," they are just "maybe." That can get frustrating when all you are wanting is a straight answer, and every time you shuffle and ask again you keep on pulling another "maybe" card. It is at times like that when my belief in the tarot is reignited because no matter how many times I ask a question, I always get the same answer.

If the answer you are looking for is tied to a certain outcome like the one mentioned above, it is also important to think about why the cards are giving you a "maybe" answer. Perhaps there is some course of action you must take first before the cards will be able to provide a more concrete answer. For example, if I asked about becoming a tarot reader but I was doing nothing to market myself or make it known that I read tarot, then why would the cards say yes? Sometimes we must take action first.

By using the tarot cards to explore our own feelings, we can begin to see a different side of ourselves. Just like the tarot portrays the Fool's journey, which is said to be the journey of an individual as they go through the stages of life or magickal apprenticeship to achieve new levels of consciousness, the tarot can also show the afterlife. The saying rings true: "as above, so below." You could begin to ask yourself, What if the Fool really did fall from the cliff? What then? What journey is this telling us about? This is why I think it can be beneficial to read *The Egyptian Book of the Dead* and see what imagery comes up for you in relation to the tarot cards. While you're at it, don't be afraid to shuffle some cards around; you may find that a different order works better. This concept reminds us that there are multiple sides, or a shadow realm, to the tarot, just as there is the shadow part of us. The royals of the tarot may hold their own keys to a part of your shadow. Below is a journaling exercise to help you explore.

EXERCISE
JOURNALING WITH THE ROYALS

This exercise with the tarot is something that I suggest you take your time with. It doesn't have to be done all in one day, one week, or even one month. It is a slow process, and each time you return to it, it may reveal more to you. Each time you revisit a single card, more parts of that card jump out at you, like the little rabbit in the Queen of Pentacles card.

You will need:
- Pen and paper or journal
- The Kings and Queens of each suit

The steps:
When you're ready, pull each of the royal cards and go through the journaling prompts for each card. Write down whatever comes into your mind; let it flow. By going through this exercise, you may uncover something that has been just under the surface for a while.

King and Queen of Cups:
- When something bothers me, how do I deal with it? Do I talk about it, write about it, deal with it alone?
- When I have strong emotions, what do I do to work through them currently?
- Are my emotions easily influenced?
- How did I learn to deal with my emotions as a child?
- What is one thing I can do for myself when I am sad, angry, or frustrated?
- Do I allow myself to celebrate when something good happens? Why or why not?
- When someone angers me, what do I do? How do I handle the situation?
- How do I use my magick when I am feeling low?
- How do I use my magick to celebrate?

King and Queen of Swords:
- How am I taking care of my thoughts each day?
- How much time do I spend without my phone or any devices? How am I letting myself just be free to think and observe my own thoughts?

- What do I do currently when I have a negative thought?
- What steps can I take in the future when I have a negative or limiting thought?
- How have my thoughts shaped who I am today?
- How quickly do I look at my phone or other devices each morning? Can I give myself more time in between waking up and going on my devices in order to be in my own thoughts or meditate?
- How have I learned to set boundaries? What does setting a boundary look like for me?
- Am I closed off to meeting new people or do I welcome it? If I have walls around me, where did they come from? When do they serve me and when do they not?
- What is the way I communicate best? Now that I understand this, how is this going to help me move forward?

King and Queen of Wands:
- How am I taking care of my body each day?
- Am I listening to my body? How does it talk to me?
- How am I nourishing my body each day? What stops me from doing this?
- When does my body feel best and why? When does it feel worst and why?
- When I get excess energy, what do I do with it? (Walk, play a sport, create?)
- When I get an idea, how quickly do I take action? Am I impulsive or do I take my time and plan everything out?
- How can my magick also help my body?

- What parts of my body need more love?
- How can I thank my body for being my earthly home and housing all of this magick?

King and Queen of Pentacles:
- How does my space reflect how I am feeling? Does it get easily cluttered? Is it organized?
- How does my space reflect me as an individual? What story does it tell?
- How do I use my magick in my space? What kind of cleansing do I do? Have I done any protection magick or banishing?
- Do I feel good when I buy something new for myself? Or do I regret it?
- How do I feel about having a savings account? Am I okay with it starting small and growing over time?
- Do I welcome opportunities for abundance? Why or why not?
- When I get a new opportunity, is it easy for me to accept the benefits or do I try to self-sabotage?
- Do I feel worthy of being comfortable in life? Why or why not?
- What is my favorite way of treating myself when I am able to?

* * *

The journal prompts are meant to be a chance to explore without judgment the way that each of the elements works in our lives and how we allow them to work in our lives. It's not about feeling bad or calling yourself out for being unbalanced in a certain area. Everything is always changing; there is a constant ebb and flow of the elements throughout our lives. I don't believe that anyone will ever have a perfect balance of all the elements in their life, as perfection doesn't exist. In nature, everything is chaotic yet somehow works together seamlessly, like the mechanics of a clock. It is okay if life feels chaotic; you can use that chaos and channel it for your magick.

EXERCISE
MAKING A ROYAL DECISION

Consulting the tarot for decisions in our lives is one of the most common ways that the tarot can be used. Within the tarot community there has been some debate about whether one should ask the tarot yes or no questions. Perhaps this is because a yes or no answer is seen as definitive. I personally think a yes or no answer is more fluid and allows us to understand both our question and what we actually want on a deeper level. Isn't it true that when you go to ask the question, you already have the desired outcome in your mind? You will want one of the answers to come through. This shows which way you are personally leaning, which could give you more of an answer than the tarot itself. There is also the possibility that you need to change something in order to get your desired outcome. If the tarot comes back with a no, then it is not set in stone; it is fluid, and you can change the response by changing something you are currently doing. Yes or no questions are more like loose guides than cemented signposts. Whether you agree with asking the tarot yes or no questions, just one card can reveal an answer. It is important to remember that you are the magick and that you hold the power. The cards are a tool for you to explore your own decisions and to help you understand the next right action to take; they aren't there to make all of your decisions for you. Never give your power up to something, even if it is a divinatory tool. Here's a quick spread for decision-making using the royal cards.

You will need:
- The royal cards from a tarot deck (Kings and Queens)

The steps:
1. Begin with your question in mind.
2. Shuffle the eight cards.
3. When you are ready, pull two cards and lay them beside each other.
4. The first card will give you general guidance about the decision. It might reveal whether it will be emotional, energetic, financial, or spiritual in nature. It will also reveal what needs to be explored or removed before you can make a proper decision.
5. The second card will reveal the steps you need to take and could provide the potential outcome of the decision.
6. Because we are working with the royal cards, they will be full of energy, but you will also need to spend some time meditating on each card, looking at the element, the scenery, and feeling the overall energy.

Allow yourself to take some time. It is okay to leave the cards and return to them a few hours later, as sometimes this reveals new levels of information. Regardless, your intuition should tell you all you need to know once the cards have been pulled.

* * *

KEYS TO WISDOM

Using the royal cards when it comes to self-love work is both an empowering and humbling experience. It is one that can lead you to having a stronger connection to the voice of the true self within. The Kings and Queens of the tarot are in an interesting position. They all hold their own kind of wisdom and face their own challenges. To understand them is to understand ourselves, and so is the case with each of the tarot cards. To be unapologetically magick is to be unapologetically royal in your own life.

Chapter 6
EVERYDAY MAGICK

Throughout the larger occult community, you may run into people who don't like the idea of "everyday magick." This generally means magick that doesn't require a lot of preparation time or an intense ritual-like experience. It's magick that is sourced from objects or habits in your daily life. There may be people who feel that magick requires a lot of setup and takedown. And yes, I agree that there is much to be gained from a well-thought-out ritual or a ceremony with your peers, but magick comes in many forms, and everyday magick is still magick.

In this chapter, I'm going to talk about everyday magick as the things we do throughout the day—things that are so small sometimes we don't even recognize them as magick. When I refer to ritual magick, I am going to be referring to the more elaborate and planned-out ceremonies and spells that one might conduct for something special. Both everyday magick and ritual magick work together, and you will often find throughout your own practice that some days, some weeks, or some full moons you just won't feel like planning something big, and it's important during those times to remember that magick is what you make of it and doesn't require any fancy tools or fancy performances. This is not to say that ritual magick doesn't have its time and place; it certainly does, which is why we need to talk about them both.

It is important to mention that one is not better than the other. As I noted in the first chapter, magick is available to us all the time because we are the best tools we have. If we needed specific tools, the right time of day, the best possible location, or any other thing to make magick work for us, then it wouldn't really be all that empowering. Sure, correspondences for days of the week or candle colors or anything else can be helpful, but if we depend upon these things all the time, I truly believe it takes away from our own power and our own ability to wield magick at any time, in any place, from nothing but ourselves.

MAGICK IN THE MUNDANE

On any given night of the week, you'll find me in line at the grocery store being a semi-responsible adult by making sure I have food in my fridge. To be honest, I hate grocery shopping, but I force myself to do it. Every time I think the parking lot looks too busy, I start to get anxious. When I first started to dive into the wonderful world of magick, I thought I was going to be meditating six hours a day and live in my own little magickal world. I came to realize that even though I can practice magick, I still live in the real world and deal with real problems. I realized that I needed magick to be able to help me with the mundane. After all, if magick can't help me live a little better, then what is it here for? That's when I decided to start using my magick to help me on my grocery store trips. I would begin to pray and bless myself before I left and then send myself a text message with a protection spell in it; that way I would carry it with me wherever I went because I don't go anywhere without my phone.

When my grandmother died, I decided to take a death doula course. My course came with the book *The Art of Death Midwifery* by Joellyn St. Pierre. Within the book, one of the passages struck me as an honest representation of what it means to be a practitioner of magick. It read, "It is important that we remember that *we* are not healers. We are guides and conduits. Through aligning our will with divine will, divine healing may flow, but that healing, being perfect to the individual, can take many forms."[13] We are all conduits of energy, and we can wield it however we like. I used to be worried when something in my life was going too well or when a spell I cast came to fruition too quickly. "It's too good to be true," I thought. Of course, my worrying would cause me to change my energy, and something would happen. I suppose it was a self-fulfilling prophecy. It wasn't until I realized that I *am* magick, therefore magick is working through me all the time, that I began to worry less about the outcome and more about how I was empowering myself.

One of the best days of the past year that I can remember was a day when I wasn't feeling all the best. There was no rhyme or reason; I just wasn't feeling like myself. I decided to do something I had never done before, and I took a walk in the sun and bought myself a birthday cake on a day that wasn't my birthday. It cost me only a few dollars, and it made me happy for the rest of the day, and I wondered why I had waited twenty-nine years to step outside of the birthday box and buy a decorated cake. It seems so silly to me now to wait 364 days to get a cake with decorated frosting. That day I took it home, lit the birthday candles, and made a wish. It was a small act but a very large spell, and

---

13. Joellyn St. Pierre. *The Art of Death Midwifery: An Introduction and Beginner's Guide* (San Bernadino, CA: Booksurge, 2020), 26.

one that I would consider everyday magick. It's true that wishes upon birthday cakes are a form of magick; they require intention, energy, and trust in the universe to carry out said wish, and more people should be using them on more days than just the big one.

When we think about candle magick, we often think about seven-day glass candles or handcrafted candles rolled in herbs, but I think the tiny birthday candles that we stick on top of cakes can also do the trick and can be easily found at your local dollar store. What about starting your morning with a wish? A wish is the perfect form of everyday magick because it carries hope and opens the door for possibility. Next time you have your morning coffee, try setting up a birthday candle. You can light the bottom of it until the wax gets hot and stick it on a small glass plate or candleholder. Next, set an intention for the day and say something like, "I wish for a good and magick-filled day where anything is possible." You could get more concrete by saying, "Today will be a good day, so mote it be." Then, blow out the candle. There you have it; you don't need a birthday to make a wish on a small candle.

Some forms of everyday magick aren't so easily recognized. Now, this example might seem a little silly, but it did do something for me! Right now on social media, it is popular to use trending sounds in videos that you share with your audience. As I was scrolling through my social platform one day, I heard a sound that talked about changing your behavior in the present so that it didn't create problems for your future self. *Aha!* I thought that was pure gold. Immediately I began to think about all of the patterns that keep recurring in my life, the ones that I tell myself I will "fix tomorrow." I got up from my chair and took an erasable marker to all the mirrors in my home, writing that phrase down. I wanted to remind myself that I could change the things I didn't like, such as my habit to procrastinate or the fact that I don't exercise regularly. I started to use the phrase to empower myself on a daily basis.

EXERCISE
DAILY EMPOWERMENT

Words are powerful; we know this! It's time to start using it to our advantage daily so that we can get the most out of them.

You will need:
- A dry-erase marker
- A whiteboard (optional)
- A pen and paper or a way to record your thoughts

The steps:
1. Begin in a comfortable position. Take a few deep breaths and smile.

2. Begin to think about how you want to feel each day and what words would make you feel that way. I usually want to feel empowered and confident. We won't be able to feel good every day, but we can at least set ourselves up for success on our end.

3. Write down all the words that make you feel whatever feeling you have chosen.

4. Now create one to two sentences using some of those words. These will be sentences that you won't mind seeing every day.

5. If you are able, write that sentence with your dry-erase marker wherever you are most likely to see

it. It could be the mirror, the window, the fridge, etc. Just make sure that it is a surface that is easily cleaned so as to allow you to erase the sentence when you want.

6. Say the sentence out loud to yourself. Each day when you come across the sentence, wherever you have written it, say it out loud to yourself and remember that you are worth it.

∗ ∗ ∗

ART MAGICK

Another form of everyday magick is undeniably art. Throughout history there have been many witches and occultists who turned to art to express their practice. There is something purely divine about the very act of creating something. The time spent creating by putting pen or paintbrush to paper, knitting, molding clay, or doing any other type of art is time that you are actively bringing something into existence by sheer will. There is also something very sacred about bringing the Witches' Pyramid into the process of art.

The Witches' Pyramid takes the practitioner through four stages: to know, to will, to dare, and to keep silent.[14] I used to always think that if I created something I had to share it with someone or it wasn't real. If it was only for myself, it felt like a waste of time and energy. By applying the Witches' Pyramid to the act of creating art, I was able to go deeper and create something that truly represented a piece of me. I didn't have to worry about how others would react

---

14. Éliphas Lévi, *Transcendental Magic: Its Doctrine and Ritual*, trans. Arthur Edward Waite (London: William Rider & Son, Limited, 1923), 37.

or if they would enjoy it; I was able to explore myself and create magick.

There is also something very potent about channeling energy while creating art. I believe a lot of artists do it, whether they pull ideas from the idea highway or the ideas rise up from inside the depths of their bellies. You could very well turn a piece of art into a home for a servitor or a channeled spirit. Your art could represent the energy you felt in that moment or be the storehouse for an energy you wish to continue working with, allowing you to access that energy every time you revisit that painting. Many artists also hide different symbols or sigils within their work. A sigil is an image created from a word or string of words that relate to an intention or desired outcome. The sigil is usually charged and used for creating the wanted change. Later in the book there is a step-by-step guide on how to create a sigil. For now, this could be something to consider when creating art. If you created a painting and while working on it set the intention that it was for protection so that when you hung it up at home it warded off negative and malevolent energies, then you could also create a sigil and place that into your painting. Just think about how many paintings or artistic images you've seen with sigils and didn't even realize it!

RITUALS FOR SILLY THINGS

As noted at the beginning of the chapter, when we think of rituals, we often think that they need to be for serious things. We can trick ourselves into thinking that we need a solid occasion for them or that we need a certain set of materials. Yes, rituals that require a lot of work and special materials and the right moon phase and the right words intoned do provide us with something very moving and very enriching. But, dare I say, sometimes a ritual can be done on a whim, and it can be done for a very silly reason. There is something Divine about being able to laugh at yourself and simply have some fun.

What I love about rituals is that they create an atmosphere. If they were a form of entertainment, they would be an evening showing at a theater. Rituals offer a chance to completely take the consciousness into the energy you are creating. They can offer a very transformative experience, and through ritual many lessons can be taught. There is often an ebb and flow to ritual. You may find at one moment you are full of energy and expressive, at another time you may feel calm and still.

The fun thing about rituals is that you can create them yourself. Every single aspect of them can be your own piece of dramatic art. Imagination is the best guide when it comes to creating and carrying out a ritual. You could create one that honors one of your favorite movie characters and helps you to study the archetype that they represent. You could create a ritual for honoring a certain phase that your life has passed through. This could also be a ritual for letting go of something that you have been carrying with you but you know you are ready to move on from.

Alternatively, many people have daily rituals that they swear by. These are small things like having a care routine after showering. This might involve putting on lotion, perfume, brushing your hair, etc., and as you do these things you say positive affirmations for your day. Someone else could have a ritual of drinking their morning coffee on their porch and sitting quietly to contemplate gratitude. You could have a date with yourself one evening a week where you lay out some tarot cards, have a cup of tea, and divine messages, each time using the same teacup, kind of tea, and tarot deck to do so. I would argue that if you have a favorite movie and each year you decide to take the time to watch it, and before pressing play you prepare your space and during the movie you consciously pull useful messages from it, that would be an annual ritual—especially if the movie helps you to learn something or transforms you in some way. Each year that you revisit the movie, you'll remember your previous lessons while being open to receiving new ones. Allow yourself to try something simply for the sake of having the experience. When we let go of needing to have an outcome and allow the ritual to be what it is, strange and beautiful things tend to happen.

MAGICK DURING WONKY TIMES

Not every day is going to be a good day; that's just how life is. We're human and some days are just going to suck—sometimes whole weeks or months are going to suck—and it is during these times that our magick can be one of our greatest tools, helping us to make it through. Magick, in my humble opinion, should be accessible because if you always need to have the perfect conditions, the right altar setup, the most glamorous tools, or pray for sixty consecutive days before casting a spell … that's not going to be achievable for most people. Sure, you could argue that by requiring certain things it would make people "work" for it and therefore they would learn discipline or their tools and practice would be imbued with more energy.

I am not saying that long rituals that require intense focus and dedication don't matter; I believe they do and that they work, but that doesn't mean we should keep our magick in a walled garden until the time is right. It is when life feels unbearable and lonely and utterly exhausted of any meaning that we need magick the most. Being unapologetically magick isn't believing in some fairy tale where we can snap our fingers and everything magickally falls back into place; it is taking responsibility for our own power and our own place in the world and owning that even when things get tough.

Your practice can also be a place of rest when you need it most. Many, many times I have gone to the altar to cry and pray and have been consoled by spirit. Your practice can become part of the foundation, something for the rest of your life to build upon, rather than some kind of side dish. Like I mentioned in the introduction, it isn't about screaming your practice from the rooftops and letting everyone know what you're up to; it's about having something sacred that is for you and will be there for you when the world gets wonky.

The world is already pretty wonky on its own, but there are things that happen like divorce, miscarriages, death, breaking up with a friend—all things that can cause hurt and pain in our lives. Magick will not fix everything, but a spiritual practice can be a home during the good times and the bad. If it doesn't feel like home, it's time to ask yourself why. Sometimes it could be because we haven't settled into our practice enough. In the digital age, this might be more of an issue, as people may feel pressured to share their practice online in order to socialize. This is fine, but one could run the risk of always posting online and never working the practice outside of the digital sphere. With social media today there is a lot to compare yourself and your practice to, and that itself can become a cycle of not feeling good enough.

If your practice doesn't feel like home, it could also be because you haven't experimented with it enough. Give it some time, stretch out the corners, don't keep it in a box just because that is what is expected of you. No, a magick spell will not take away the pain of a broken heart, but it could open the path to healing.

Magick is a tool that can help us if we are willing to help ourselves. Often in our lives there will be doors we automatically close without thinking; perhaps it is because we have not yet gained the confidence needed to keep them open or the self-esteem to feel we deserve to have them open.

The same idea holds true with other things in our lives. Take the prior example of a broken heart: if you were to cast a spell to ease the heartache of losing a lover, the magick could take place in many forms. New friends could come into your life, you might be invited somewhere fun for a weekend, your sibling might offer a good therapist, or you might hear about a new hobby that sounds interesting. All of these things could be beneficial to someone looking to discover themselves again after a breakup, but unless the individual is willing to take some initiative and keep the pathway of healing open, the spell will have little to work with in order to generate any success.

Of course, life comes at us in waves, and our magick must adjust to the ebbs and flows. Life is not going to be peachy all the time, and sometimes we will simultaneously want our spell to work, while another part of ourselves will not. It is at these times that you must give yourself some grace. It is okay if something starts to work and you shut the door out of fear. You are the magick, and you can do it again, only this time you'll know to keep the door open.

The same is true for our overall practice. There will be times when you feel very in tune and aligned with your practice. You may get into a steady routine of pulling a tarot card daily or praying often or frequently walking in nature. Then, there may be other times when you haven't touched your tarot cards in weeks and your prayer game hasn't been that strong either, or you can't remember the last time you cleansed the house. Don't beat yourself up during these times; we all go through the flows of life, and your practice is with you through it all. Even when things get a bit crooked, know that your own personal practice, outside of social media, outside of other people's opinions, outside of your own self-doubt, is there and it will always be there. Magick was made for wonky times.

Chapter 7
ALCHEMY OF APPEARANCE

I love experimenting with what I wear and doing my makeup. Experimenting with my appearance has quickly become one of my favorite magickal instruments and a way to express myself and heal. I don't think aesthetic or fashion needs to be expensive, and I do most of my shopping at the thrift store, where I can find items for as little as a few dollars. Many witches and magickal practitioners find comfort in changing the look and feel of their altar based on the Wheel of the Year, and others like to redecorate and do a full cleanse on each month's new moon. Fashion, accessories, and makeup can be used in much the same way. You can experiment with maximalism or minimalism; you can play with colors or try a monochrome look. You can become a piece of art, your own object of devotion, a testament to all you have been through and what you want to express to the world.

You can be a collection of items, with each piece specially curated. Experimenting with style is taking your will, creating something out of it, and changing the way you feel, think, or experience something. Fashion is totally a form of magick. Let's explore personal style as a tool in our magickal tool kit.

STYLE AS A MAGICKAL TOOL

It doesn't have to be difficult to have a great style or your own unique way of dressing. It also doesn't have to cost a lot or take up a lot of your time. The way that we dress can change the way we feel, walk, and even behave. I'm sure at one time or another we have all felt like a badass after putting on a fresh outfit. Clothes can hold power, but it is important to remember that the power they hold ultimately comes from ourselves.

I have found that the more I experiment and the more I try to step out of the house with something a little more daring, the more confidence I have in my own sense of style. Although, this isn't easy, and there are still days when I have to gear myself up with a little pep talk before opening the door. If you are someone who wants to start experimenting but you are nervous about the response you might get from others or you are feeling self-conscious about it, there are a few things you can do to ease the transition.

1. Begin to wear the clothes, accessories, or makeup that you feel best in around your house first. This will give you a chance to experiment in the comfort of your own space.

2. Start small when you do begin to venture outside. Maybe this means dressing as you normally would but adding a small accessory like a necklace, earrings, hat, boots, etc. The whole outfit doesn't need to change drastically overnight; you can begin by adding pieces until you feel confident to step out fully.

3. Check in with yourself and what you are thinking and feeling. Although it can seem a bit frightening when finally trying something new, often our true self knows

what we want and that we are capable of achieving it. By checking in with yourself you are taking a moment to breathe and come back to alignment with why you are beginning to experiment with your appearance in the first place. Chances are, if this chapter resonates with you, it is because you want to start expressing yourself in this way, and that is a deeply beautiful thing!

Experimenting with your own personal style will take some time, especially if you haven't really done it before, and that is okay. Knowing that it will take time and that you don't need to rush will help you on your journey. I have personally found taking it slow to be beneficial, as I tend to lean more toward a maximalist style. I can't get enough of tulle skirts, layers of necklaces, loud makeup, funky accessories, and mixed and matched patterns. I want to walk out of the house with the whole damn closet on. But, of course, it takes time to work up the confidence! Recognize how brave you are for taking the chance and congratulate yourself for doing it.

Finding Your Personal Style

As someone who loves to experiment, I can go from artsy to grunge to vintage quick. I love to change up my look and pull from different style genres, but I always have a few that I go back to again and again. If I had to choose just one, I would go with a maximalist grunge look. Don't be pressured into feeling like you must choose one aesthetic and stick with it. Freedom lies in being able to try new things and find what you love. There are many people I know who don't have an "on brand" aesthetic but choose to live each day as a new style adventure, and I love that!

Every style can be a spell, and we can choose our style based on what we are wanting for the day. Personal style lines up with the *intention* and *belief* part of spellwork. If you are someone who likes to mix different aesthetics, you can create a look based on intention. Think about what you would like to do that day—maybe it is to boost your confidence, elevate your mood, or simply feel comfortable. If you are using fashion as a form of self-love, you can keep that intention with you while you choose your clothing.

One of my favorite ways to get inspiration for looks is to create style boards. The old-school way of making a style board is to cut out pictures from magazines and make a style collage on paper. I used to have a notebook full of style collages, and I would design clothes for paper dolls. I remember having a little book of cutout clothes and sitting in the living room dressing my paper doll.

Today we live in a tech world, and making inspirational style boards has never been easier. There are many photo apps that allow you to save and name collections of pictures. I mostly use Pinterest and save style inspiration to different style boards. In each of my boards, I have pictures of full looks, clothes, crafts, and even home décor because you never know what kind of inspiration you can pull from and add into your own wardrobe. The boards will be another place to keep our collections and another place to show off our personal style, although if you choose not to use technology in your practice, it is never a requirement.

Having style boards is great because you can easily keep all your aesthetics organized, and you can pull from each one to make your own unique style. I also love finding inspiring people to follow. One of them runs a shop called Funky Grunge Boutique, and all of their clothing and accessories come with an artistic flare that is specially handcrafted.

Another thing to consider is exploring a fashion philosophy. This is often a reason for wearing the clothes that you do, having a *why* to your outfit or personal style. Having a personal fashion philosophy is optional, and if you choose to incorporate one into the way you dress, it may take some time to develop. I like the grunge philosophy of thrifting and not needing expensive items to have style, but you may like a different philosophy that says you deserve to take up space and be bold. Take time to look at different fashion theories and philosophies and see which ones resonate with you.

Finally, when creating a personal style, I like to find alternative sources for inspiration. Creating your own Book of Muse is a fun thing. This is a journal specifically for fashion inspiration, and in it you write a sentence or two every time something inspires you. It's basically a giant list that you can call upon any time you want! In my Book of Muse, I have characters from movies, song lyrics, feelings from paintings, lines of poetry, random ideas, and so on. I will even write down if I become inspired by the pattern on a tablecloth or certain flowers when they are in season. Anything can offer inspiration that you can then turn into your own style.

EXERCISE
CREATE YOUR BOOK OF MUSE

This is a super fun and explorative exercise, so take your time in creating it. You could even wait until a moon phase that you feel speaks to you. Personally, I have a real love for the waning cycle of the moon; something about it disappearing speaks to my soul.

You will need:

- A pen
- A journal
- Art items (stickers, markers, glue, buttons, etc.)

The steps:

1. Get comfortable and prepare to create a book full of inspiration. This will be something that you can turn to when you want to get ideas for your fashion, but it can also assist you when you want to surf the cosmic waves of art, life, and magick. It can be a book that holds all of the things that spark joy or meaning for you when you need them.

2. Take a moment to cherish the journal. I know that might sound a little silly, but this really will be something that holds a lot of meaning for you. Say hello to it, welcome it into your life, then set its intention. You can say something like, "This is my sacred Book of Muse; it will hold all of the things that make my heart sing, it will be a steady stream connecting me to all of the people, places, and things that inspire me, it will hold and provide for me a potent and creative energy every time I open it."

3. Now, you can write on the inside of the first page a dedication to yourself. You might write something like, "I dedicate this book to the creative within me. I dedicate this book to all of the creatives that have come before me." You can include a favorite quote or poem as well.

4. Take some time to decorate the outside of the journal if you like. For my Book of Muse, I decorated the front with stickers, magazine cutouts, and quotes. This is your muse! Make it as unique as you want.

5. If you already know some of the things that inspire you or you have some ideas, you can begin to add them as bullet points or full sentences. Personally, I like to number them so when the book is full, I can see the vast number of things that have inspired me from start to finish. It might also be a good idea to include the date of when certain things have inspired you as well. You can pull in poems, quotes from people or movies that have inspired or spoken to you, art, literature, songs, sceneries, tarot cards, animals, flowers, and plants. Find the inspiration wherever it meets you.

6. Finally, put it in a safe space and return to it when you have a new idea to add or when you need some style inspiration. Keep it by your closet, in your dresser, on your shelf, on your beauty stand, on your altar if you're working some glamour magick— wherever you feel it will be safe and work for you.

* * *

ACCESSORIES

Accessories are something that people either love or they can do without. I, personally, am a fan of earrings, necklaces, belts, and bags that have a unique flair to them. I don't like wearing a lot of rings or bracelets, but that's just my preference. Accessories offer a way to add something to an outfit, and they also offer another layer of self-expression. You can choose your jewelry like you choose a tea blend: to suit the day, your mood, or what you are wanting to do in a magickal sense. Much of the jewelry that I own I found at the thrift shop, through other magickal shops, or online if something really spoke to me. I have a blend of really simple statement pieces and big, bold chunky pieces. I don't shy away from mixing colors together, and I can jump between a maximalist approach, adding several necklaces, or being more minimalist with my jewelry by just wearing one necklace and a set of earrings.

When I get something from the thrift shop, I have a little ritual I like to do. I know that the jewelry came from someone and that they probably loved it while they owned it. I try to think of who might have had it, and then I cleanse it. Sometimes beforehand I will even wash it or sanitize it, especially if I purchased a pair of earrings from the thrift shop. So in that case, I will spray it with some antiseptic spray, wipe it down with an alcohol wipe, or soak it in hot water. To cleanse, I will usually run it through the smoke of an incense stick, and then I place it on my altar and welcome it into the family! (The family being all of my other jewelry.)

I am a mood selector. What I mean is, I select jewelry by the mood I'm in. I rarely go off of whether the color or look of it aligns with the rest of my outfit. I go with what I'm feeling for that day, and that's how I tend to purchase my jewelry also. As for the magickal aspect of jewelry, that is where it can get very personal, and each individual will use, work, and wear their jewelry differently. I have a few necklaces that are strictly tied to my spiritual practice because they are occult symbols. If you are choosing to wear occult symbols, make sure to do some research on what they represent, but I'm sure if you're making the step to purchase jewelry, you've done that. Other pieces, I wear when I want to feel a certain way. Some make me feel confident, fun, funky, grunge, polished, or professional. This is a very simple but profound part of magick: changing the way you feel and embodying that feeling for the day.

If you want to choose a specific magickal purpose for a piece of jewelry, you can do that and turn it into a talisman. A talisman can be made by charging an object and consecrating it, which makes a necklace, ring, earrings, or any other accessory perfect for becoming a magickal tool.

EXERCISE
CREATE A MAGICKAL TALISMAN

You will remember that in the beginning of the book we created a good luck talisman. This talismanic exercise will require less materials but will be equally potent, and as you wear your jewelry, it will continue to work for you and connect with your energy.

You will need:
- A piece of jewelry or other accessory that you want to hold a specific magickal purpose

The steps:
1. Choose your piece of jewelry and its specific purpose. This could be to help you feel powerful, for protection, to help with charisma, or anything else you desire to use it for.

2. Take a few moments to center yourself. Close your eyes and breathe in on a count of four, hold the breath for a moment, and then exhale slowly on a

count of four. Do this four times while preparing to charge your talisman with energy.

3. Next, hold the talisman in your hands with the left hand underneath and the right hand on top. Imagine a beam of light coming down the top of your head, through the middle of your body, and down through your feet. Feel the surge of energy that this light provides. Begin to focus on your intention.

4. Now say out loud your intention. It could be something like, "I charge this magickal talisman with the power of [protection]. May it be aided by the angels Michael, Uriel, Raphael, and Gabriel. May the energy that I consecrate its body with hold true and [protect] me all the days I wear it. So it is."

5. Imagine the beam of light flowing down your arms, through your hands, and into the talisman. Hold it there for a moment and picture it being fully immersed with light and energy.

6. Now you can put the jewelry on or place it somewhere for safekeeping. Clap your hands together three times to cut the energy. Return to your talisman when you need it.

* * *

As for other accessories that you could include in your magickal fashion choices, there are a few that I'd love to present. Most of the time when I think of accessories, my mind goes to jewelry, but there are others that can add to an outfit or be charged for magickal use.

Other types of accessories:

- Socks
- Shoelaces
- Charms
- Buttons
- Embroidery
- Fabric paint
- Fabric patches
- Buttons
- Hair pins
- Glasses charms
- Sunglasses
- Wigs
- Others (Get experimental with it! Doll-part earrings, clothing pins, coins, crowns, etc.)

Accessories are a ton of fun and totally magickal. If you get to adding them into your style, I hope you find immense joy in it and that you find your unique brand of fashion along the way.

BODY POSITIVITY

Talking about style as a spell can also be anxiety inducing for some, and by "some," I mean myself. My body is bigger, and I no longer fit into many of the clothes I used to. This stopped me from experimenting with my style and wearing what I really wanted to for a long time. I felt self-conscious, and every time I put on a new outfit, I would have this voice in the back of my head telling me that I wasn't good enough. This also happens when I am thrifting; sometimes that voice will come back and tell me that my clothes don't measure up to others'. The thing is, I don't even know who these "other" people are. There are a lot of emotions that can come up when experimenting with style as a form of spellwork, and these emotions can happen for all people and all body types. Give yourself the grace to work through it and be proud of yourself for taking even the smallest step toward having fun with your style. I cannot say that it is always easy, but that is what has helped me. Don't ever feel like you need to spend money on expensive clothing or accessories just for the sake of magick or to fit in, or anything of that sort. Many of the items I wear today came from the thrift shop. It is not about the amount of money something is worth; it is about how it makes you feel.

When I first wanted to start experimenting with clothes, I went online and looked for other people who had bodies like mine. I'm happy to say that today there are more people in the fashion industry who are normalizing all types of bodies, including disabled bodies and all sizes. I think we are slowly moving in a more positive direction. I found creators with fashion accounts that were sharing plus-size clothing hauls and talking openly about the struggles they faced finding clothing that fit. It was really great to see how they put their outfits together, and it made me feel more confident about wearing the clothing I wanted to instead of hiding behind oversized T-shirts. (Although there is something fun about oversized tees!) Plus, it got a lot easier in the summer because I had a whole bunch of inspiration. When the summers would hit, I used to continue to wear long sleeves and pants, and it was really hard because everyone would be out enjoying themselves and I would be all covered up. Again, nothing wrong with covering up during the summer months, but I personally wanted to wear shorts and dresses. I can't say it was easy, but finding inspiration in other people, I was able to buy summer clothes like shorts and tops and put outfits together that

I liked and that looked good on my body. Each day is a journey, but I do feel more confident now. It didn't require losing weight or hiding behind the fabric; it was more of a mindset shift once I found other people who embraced and loved their bodies as they were. Fashion is not about hiding behind clothes; it's about embracing who we are and showing more of who we are to the world.

If you're like me and you struggle with anxiety over … everything, I have found that self-love affirmations and very short meditations do help. They are something you can say throughout the day. It doesn't have to be a big ritual or anything, but if you ever find yourself struggling through loving yourself and your body, it is something you can do in the moment. Here's my latest go-to meditation.

EXERCISE
SELF-LOVE MEDITATION

You might find this exercise a little cliché, but I have found that in the act of doing this meditation regularly a lot of the apprehension toward it faded. The more I affirmed to myself that I did indeed love myself for who I was in the moment despite my mistakes, failures, and faults, the more I began to grow in confidence, and it has allowed me to better connect with other people. It is a small meditation, but if practiced regularly, the benefits of doing so add up.

You will need:
- Just yourself, nothing else is required

The steps:

1. Say this quietly to yourself. If you are alone and somewhere quiet, you can always close your eyes and find a comfortable place to sit for a few minutes.

2. Begin by taking three deep breaths.

3. Then say out loud or internally, "I love you. I love my body that nurtures me in all of its changing forms. We are not enemies. Thank you. I am not ashamed of my body. I am proud, I am loved, I am beautiful, I am worthy."

4. Take a moment to believe it. Yes, believe it. It can be really hard, I know this, especially if you have so much negative self-talk running through your head all day. Sometimes it is easy to feel like you are covered in negative emotions all directed at yourself. This time is a brief moment for you to just love yourself, even if you have trouble doing it for the rest of the day. We all need that.

5. Open your eyes if you had them closed and continue on about your day. Self-love meditation for a moment was achieved!

* * *

AFFORDABLE FASHION

Before moving on, I also want to touch on personal style from the perspective of someone with a low income. Just because I am not able to buy all the latest trends (whether one ethically should or shouldn't is another story), or whether I can or can't afford a certain accessory doesn't mean that what I own right now shouldn't still be magickal. This isn't about going out and buying everything new to create a spell with your clothes. Your clothes can be magickal right now, just as they are, because *you* are magickal just as you are. As I sit here and type this, I am wearing an old baggy T-shirt and some leggings, and if I wanted to, I could enchant these pieces to help me embody my magick and maybe even get more writing done today. Why? Because they are what I'm going to be wearing all day, and I can wear them much like you would an enchanted piece of jewelry. Of course, if I really wanted to just throw the whole thing out the window, I could be just as magical typing here naked. The clothes don't make the witch, but when we need them, they are a nice tool to work with.

EVERYDAY SPELL FOR GLAMOUR

When I think of everyday magick, I also think of spells cast for things that I need in my life, things that have mundane purposes, and to me glamour is very much that—an everyday thing. Sure, there are parts of it that are more elaborate, but I want to take time daily to feel good about myself, and I have found glamour magick helps with this. Too often witches and magickal practitioners overlook the fact that magick can be cast for the small things in our lives just as much as the big things. We might cast a spell for a friend who asks for something but might have trouble casting one for ourselves. It can be much easier to believe that magick is going to work for someone else, and at times it can be harder to believe that it's going to work for us because we may have feelings of self-doubt or worry that we don't deserve good things. The truth is, you do deserve good things, and magick can work for you in all areas of your life.

EXERCISE

GLAMOUR SPELL FOR CONFIDENCE

Here's a prime example of a time when you can use some magick for something mundane. Let's say you have a big presentation at work in front of your boss and other leaders and you're feeling nervous. Many people are under the assumption that glamour spells are only to be used for making yourself appear in a glamourous way, but they are also used to change your tone, appearance, or energy to suit the situation at hand. In this situation, a glamour spell could be used to boost your confidence and make it through the presentation. When you're in a pinch, it's always best to speak something into existence, and if you don't have the confidence just yet, it's okay. That's why we are doing a glamour spell!

You will need:

- Nothing but yourself

The steps:

1. Think of a time when you felt your best—completely and utterly in your own lane and rocking it. Tap into that energy and feel it for a moment; close your eyes and take a deep breath in.

2. Think of someone you admire who comes across as confident and put together. Tap into their energy and feel it for a moment; close your eyes and take a deep breath in.

3. Now, having tapped into that energy, you've got to own it. Remember, if you don't believe in yourself

just yet, believe in the magick. It will carry you through.

4. Say out loud or to yourself three times over, "I am confident, I am capable, I am fearless, I am able. So it shall be."

5. Now is the time to call upon any deity you work with; you can ask them to bless you with the energy you need.

6. Thank yourself for taking the time to perform a glamour spell. Believe it, own it, know that the magick is working for you. Now get out there and show your stuff because you've just spoken your confidence into existence.

* * *

Glamour spells of this type work great for interviews, first dates, meeting new people, launching something new, or just simply starting the day and stepping out of the house. We don't need a big reason to use magick; we can use it every day in all that we do.

MAKEUP

Makeup is something that I have a huge love for and something that I have come to appreciate. My own relationship with makeup has shifted over the years. When I was younger, I used it daily as a way to hide away from the world, and if I didn't have it, I didn't like to go out. It was almost a way of staying isolated. Through many years of journaling and searching inside myself, I came to know some of the roots as to why I was using it in that way and slowly began to shift that narrative. Today I see makeup as something fun, something I enjoy but I do not need, and something that can be a magickal tool. I have also come to wear makeup that I enjoy and not makeup that someone else might enjoy. For example, I had a series of relationships where my partners would tell me I needed to wear more makeup, less makeup, certain shades of makeup, etc. I didn't like this and always felt it was a form of trying to control how I expressed myself, and so I made it a point as I got older to stay true to myself and how I chose to use makeup. I wanted to make those decisions for myself.

If you do wear makeup or want to start experimenting with it, I suggest approaching it like creating your own style. Find what inspires you and then take those inspirations and make something unique.

SIGIL MAGICK

If you wear makeup, you can also use the time it takes to apply it to work a little magick and set the intention for the day, allowing it to work for you while you wear it. The combination of makeup and sigil magick is perfect, almost like they were made for each other. In my first book, *Rise of the Witch*, I described sigil magick as "the art of using symbols to focus intent and produce magickal outcomes."[15]

Sigils are used everywhere these days whether we realize it or not—in business logos, imprinted into buildings and paintings, on websites, even added into computer and phone apps. Our signature can even be a sigil if we really want it to be. A sigil is a magickal symbol that, when charged, helps to manifest a desired outcome.

---

15. Whiskey Stevens, *Rise of the Witch: Making Magick Happen Your Way* (Woodbury, MN: Llewellyn Publications, 2021), 137.

Here's how you create a sigil:

Start with one or two sentences. Choose something that you want to bring into your life. *Example: I want to feel confident.*

Then, you will carefully remove all the vowels. (A, E, I, O, U) I usually do this by crossing them out on a piece of paper. *Example: WNT T FL CNFDNT*

Then, you will remove any repeating consonants from the sentence. *Example: WLCD*

With the remaining letters, you can play with them and rearrange them to create a symbol. It won't be a very pretty image, but if you take enough time, you could create something that looks quite magickal. It becomes the equivalent of what you are wanting to manifest.

Next, you can charge the sigil. This can be done by several methods. You can hold the symbol in your hand while chanting or repeating an affirmation. You could also use masturbation to charge the sigil, or even take the symbol itself and paint it or add it to a piece of artwork.

In order to use this sigil with makeup, I suggest drawing it on the skin with the base layer, something that can be blended once you have forged your intent and really owned the energy. Draw the sigil on your cheek with primer or foundation. Although you are going to be blending it, you will have drawn the sigil and focused your intent. By blending it and wearing it within the makeup, you will be able to keep it on as long as your makeup stays. Once you've finished applying your makeup (if you wear any), don't forget to tell yourself that *you are magick.*

If you don't wear makeup, that is fine; you can draw a sigil onto your face or body with soap while in the shower or before washing your face. Alternatively, if you use any type of body lotion, you could draw the sigil with lotion as well.

EVERYTHING YOU DO IS MAGICK

Magick is infused in all that we do, and I'm sure you have already found things throughout your daily life that it touches. By existing, noticing the "coincidences," engaging with others, and exploring your own practice, you are performing magick. By the way you speak and the thoughts you share, you are changing the world around you. Your subconscious mind is always working through you, and you can have a connection to the Divine. Don't overthink it; allow it to simply be, and all that you do will be magickal. Your fashion choices, or lack thereof, are all constructed by you. There is freedom in this because you can choose to use the alchemy of appearance anytime you need. Play with the way different appearances bring up different emotions from yourself and others. Watch how the way you dress makes you behave, walk, and act. Soon you will see the power of being able to play with how you are perceived.

Chapter 8
MAGICKAL RECORD KEEPING

Magickal record keeping might be seen as a burden by many magicians; I personally have gone through the ups and downs of the act. I have always said that it is up to the individual to choose whether they want to keep a magickal journal, and I stand by that. For surely, I do not know what is right or wrong for everyone. I also believe in exorcizing our guilt over the act of journal keeping. I am certainly not perfect in the act and have gone days, weeks, and months without keeping my journal only to feel immense guilt and regret upon returning. It is true that there's no sense in feeling terrible over something that we cannot change, but the feeling lingers nonetheless. I have found it best to simply pick up and continue onward, remembering the lesson from the previous chapter about ebbs and flows.

Through my own experience, I have found that the more "data" I can collect on myself, the better I become at handling the circumstances in my life, and I gain tremendous insights into my magickal practice. It is through the act of keeping a magickal record that one first begins to see themselves reflected on the page. Magickal record keeping can be done in several ways—through physical journaling in paper notebooks, digital journaling through computer documents, which offers the added bonus of speech to text, or through video or voice recording. I personally stick with the digital magickal record, although I do have many paper journals, which I find useful. I have many journals for many different things, but I have found for the sake of self-analysis it is easier to keep a record all in one place, allowing you to see the whole in a sort of bird's-eye view.

Many magicians might come to find that the act of keeping a magickal record has its own life, death, and rebirth. You might start off very enthusiastic about the whole thing only to become resentful of it and despise it, but if you carry on through, you might come to find a new appreciation for it and a renewed sense of interest. The only thing I have regretted more than not keeping a record is keeping the record but not putting enough information onto the page.

HOW TO BEGIN AND WHAT TO INCLUDE

A magickal journal is personal and so you should not be afraid to spill yourself onto the page unabashedly. To get down to the point of singularity, you must spill all of it out—for then you can see it all clearly and without the cage of the fragile ego. Fear will only stop you from true self-analysis and block your path as a magician or witch. You must find the courage to peer into the crevices and see what is lurking therein. Find it within yourself to record everything you can, and it will be a benefit to you down the road.

In my magickal record, I like to record these "data" points:

- Date
- Weather
- Moon phase and illumination percentage
- Mood upon waking
- Time of daily rituals

- Time of eating and what I eat
- Time of any activity and what physical activity I undertake
- Any reflections or thoughts that come to me (that seem important to record)
- Any conversations with others that feel important
- Any acts of divination
- Any experiments in a ritual or spellcasting
- Any dreams I have

These are the points that I record, but you might find new things to record to acquire more "data" on yourself. The more you record, the longer each daily journal entry becomes. In the end, it is well worth it, so if your journal entries begin as one page and then move onto two, three, or four pages, don't worry too much about that; the more information you put down, the more you will begin to see.

I have found that the struggle sometimes comes in the morning. I began to write down my mood upon waking because I wanted to be able to analyze if anything played a role in my moods from the start. I thought that there might be a relationship to my sleeping habits, eating habits, moon phase, weather, rituals, etc. What I did not expect was how hard it would be to figure out what mood I was actually in. Some days I know automatically that I feel happy or sad or worried. Other days it feels like I am feeling *something*, but I can't quite get the word for it. Through this I found something called an emotion wheel, which outlines a wide variety of emotions, more than I am going to include, but I will leave you with a list to start from. If none of these work, it's okay to write down "I don't know," and maybe you'll figure it out throughout the day; if you don't, that's okay too.

EMOTIONS

- Serenity
- Joy
- Optimism
- Interest
- Ecstasy
- Vigilant
- Panic
- Anticipation
- Rage
- Anger
- Annoyance
- Disgust
- Contempt
- Loathing
- Boredom
- Sadness
- Remorse
- Grief
- Pensiveness
- Surprise
- Amazement
- Distraction
- Disapproval
- Fear
- Terror
- Apprehension
- Trust
- Admiration
- Acceptance
- Happiness
- Loneliness

You also might find that you aren't just one emotion and that some days you are a mix of emotions. I find it easiest to sit with myself for a minute and root out which emotions I'm feeling, then I record them all. It's okay to be more than one thing, emotions included.

POTENCY

While going about my day, I run into certain pockets of thought, and during these times there are so many new ideas, insights, and revelations rushing in that if I don't write them down right away, I fear I might lose some of their potency or original meaning. Artists, creators, writers, and everyone else under the sun have had bursts of inspiration or late-night ideas that they didn't write down and regretted it shortly after. The idea of potency is to record the inspiration immediately or as soon as possible to ensure that the proper essence reveals itself through words on the page. I have found that the words themselves reveal more when the energy of the original thought is still fresh in my mind, which serves me well when I return to the page later to reflect. This, too, is not something to feel guilty about if you cannot record something immediately, but if you are performing a certain ritual, meditating, or taking on any other magickal task, it would be wise to have your magickal record nearby.

Last year, I purchased Jane Wolfe's diary collection. Through reading her diary, it was interesting to see the way she would write during her moments of meditation, especially when a symbol or image came into her mind. One of my favorite moments in the diary is when she is meditating and sees a tree, but she cannot approach the tree, and so she writes that she will "try again and look for another tree." In response, Aleister Crowley wrote back, "No, there is only one tree."[16] I think the message is significant, as it shows our tendency to look for alternative routes, but often the way to finding an answer is through persistence. If you are meditating, is each "new" tree the same as the other? Are they all an extension of you? I found the comment has given me much to think about, as I'm sure it will do the same for you.

At the moment, it might be hard to find words for what you are experiencing; this can be difficult when we are speaking the language of symbol. I have found it best during these times to not try to be perfect but to get something down into the record by

---

16. Jane Wolfe, *Jane Wolfe: The Cefalu Diaries 1920–1923*, comp. David Shoemaker (Sacramento, CA: Temple of the Silver Star, 2017), 10.

way of word or image. If you need to, you can draw what you are seeing in your mind's eye; these symbols could be a key to a future door you are going to need to unlock. It is better safe than sorry in that case, so draw it out, sound it out—do whatever needs to be done to save the information you receive; you never know when you're going to need it.

OTHER THINGS TO CONSIDER

Depending on how you are learning magick, you might find a digital record easier. I began writing my record out on physical paper because I liked the idea of keeping journals and pages together in one place. It felt very private and confidential, and it made sense seeing as I never wanted anyone else to look at them. As I progressed, I found a digital journal worked best, as typing became easier for me, and it allowed me to save certain images directly into my journal or in the same folder on my desktop. Another thing I like to do in my journals is to take photos of the tarot readings I give to myself. If you have a digital record, it is easy these days to take a photo of the cards and upload it into your journal. I have found this to be an especially rich system, as it offers incredible gains with the ability to look back at the cards months later with fresh perspective. You might even consider giving yourself a tarot reading at the beginning of each month and recording it in your journal. I have found that the ability to look back on my readings after some time has passed is very helpful, and I can see exactly what they were trying to tell me! They always say hindsight is twenty-twenty and, in that hindsight, much can be learned about one's forward direction. It is never a waste to look back at the cards to dive into the future—or more importantly, the present.

During my time of analyzing the cards, I record any insights that come to me in my record, as well as the cards and the positions themselves. At the end, I take a photo and upload it to make sure that I will be able to look back on it later. It also gives me a chance to see what I thought about the reading when it was fresh and how accurate I was. The exercise of pulling the cards and being able to revisit them later also allows you to see if you have been able to transform your circumstances or whether "fate" has played itself out through the cards.

Another interesting thing that you might consider is once you have enough "data" on yourself, you could carefully input that data into a spreadsheet and from that spreadsheet create a graph. This could give a visual representation of patterns that have occurred over a certain length of time. For the sake of reflecting on your relationships and encounters and therefore yourself, this might not be the best way to analyze those diary entries. That will take some time to see where you have been casting your own projections, where your shadow has spilled onto the page without you knowing it, and what it's all telling you. But, for things like the discovery of whether a daily ritual improves sleep habits (or something similar), a graph could give some insight. It could be interesting to look at starting times of rituals in comparison to outcomes or hours of meditation per day in comparison to mood. By keeping a daily magickal record, you will have accumulated some base data, and by seeing it visually represented, it may give you a better idea of what is working for you as an individual and what isn't.

DREAMS

I have found it very important in my own magickal practice to record the dreams that I have in my daily magickal journal. I do this because I am able to see on which date I had the dream and what may have been happening in my life on the surrounding dates. This allows me to analyze what the dream may be trying to tell me from my subconscious mind. I have regretted not writing down a dream upon waking, and to this day I wish I had on numerous occasions fought the desire to go back to bed and instead arose from a sleep-soaked state to write it all down. For example, I once had a dream that I was getting married to a man that I don't remember seeing before, my mother was walking me down the aisle, and there were so many people in attendance for the wedding. I began to get very anxious, and I turned to my mother to say, "I can't do this, the contract is binding!" As I got to the man at the end of the aisle, I looked into his eyes, and within them were two tarot cards, one of which was the Six of Swords card. This prompted me to say, "Oh, you're going on a trip anyway." When I awoke, I was still very sleepy, so I did not record my dream right away, and to this day I cannot remember the other tarot card that was in the man's eyes! If you can, try to fight against the urge to go back to bed before recording your dreams; there might be a valuable piece of information that you wish you had written down! Later in this book I will discuss why I believe dreams to be important and why they are part of an essential language.

TIME TRAVEL

The treasure of a magickal journal lies in the ability to analyze it over a period of time, have a consistent record, and find what produces the best results for oneself. I like the idea of recording for potency—in the moment and upon inspiration—because the words seem to carry a certain energy. I am under the belief that if you keep a hefty record, then you could mentally and energetically jump back into that day and into past events. Of course, all of this happens in the mind; I don't have an actual time machine, so my body stays in the present. But the act of traveling back in time through my records allows me to experience something multiple times, and by revisiting it, I might gain more knowledge and insight than if I would have just let it slip through the sand. This offers the added bonus of "playing the tape to the end" when it comes to certain magickal experiments. If you record your experiments and revisit them at a later date, you'll be able to go through the events in your mind and play out different scenarios, adding a little psychodrama to the magick! You'll be able to visualize why something didn't work *and* how it might have, which could assist you in the future should you try your experiment again.

SAMPLE JOURNAL ENTRY

I am going to give you a sample journal entry. It is made up—my own journals I usually reserve for the eyes of myself and, only occasionally, my mentor. It is important to remember that this is just an outline and that you can add more information wherever you like.

September 3rd, 2022

> *Weather:* Sunny, warmer but still cold
>
> *Moon phase:* First quarter, illumination 47%
>
> *Mood upon waking:* Anxious and a bit restless
>
> *9:00 a.m.:* LBRP. Woke up feeling very tired but didn't want to go back to sleep and ruin my sleep cycle.

9:30 a.m.: One cup of coffee with oat milk.

10:00 a.m.: Began reading *The Yoga Sutras of Patanjali.* Interesting how it is written that the yogic term for memories is "impressions."[17]

11:00 a.m.: Went for a walk to get out and get some exercise. It is good to get fresh air, and it gave me time to think about what I had been reading.

12:00 p.m.: One cup of coffee with oat milk. One glass of water. Three eggs, scrambled.

2:00 p.m.: Found myself exploring the idea of certain cosmological phenomena. Does it play a role in magick? Must remember to revisit later.

3:00 p.m.: Went for a walk with my partner. We practiced saying confident affirmations for our future. Enjoyed nature and was reminded of the importance of taking breaks and unplugging.

5:00 p.m.: One porkchop, one cup of rice, half a cup of broccoli. One glass of water. One cup Earl Grey tea with oat milk.

6:00 p.m.: Did some light reading. Thought about how books are telepathy. Revisited a conversation I had with someone where I might have been projecting my own feelings onto them. Must look at that later.

9:00 p.m.: LBRP before bed.

---

17. Sri Swami Satchidananda, *The Yoga Sutras of Patanjali* (Yogaville, VA: Integral Yoga Publications, 2012), 27.

THE POWER OF MISTAKES

Recording your mistakes and mishaps is valuable as well. Have you ever had a day where you learned something so cool and so new to you that it felt like a huge epiphany? As if it was outrageous that you hadn't known that information before and your entire world shifted? That's what it felt like when I realized that all the mistakes I've made during my spellwork were lessons in disguise.

For example, I once tried to conduct a spell for contacting the Divine. At the time, I felt like it didn't work. I felt nothing: no energy, had no thoughts come into my mind that might signify a connection... nothing. My spell had, to my own definition, failed. Over the next few days, I decided that I needed to do some research; perhaps I needed to try a new method. It was because of this apparent failure that I discovered Phil Hine's work and have come to understand chaos magick on a whole new level. On this magickal journey you might come to find that you are guided by something—this invisible source that threads together all experiences both big and small—there to teach you the lessons you're meant to learn.

In a perfect world we would conduct a spell and the outcome would happen just like that with the snap of a finger. Sometimes it does work that way; other times the outcome takes a little longer, and in my own experience, it's usually worth the wait. Other times, though, we technically might get what we wanted but the outcome looks wrong, as if something didn't happen quite right. Or better yet, sometimes the exact opposite of what we were spellcasting for happens. It's in these times that it is super important not to get discouraged—well, you can be discouraged for a little while, that's normal, but don't stop working your magick just because something didn't turn out right the first time.

Your daily magickal record is the perfect place to record any spells because you will be recording the time, the date, and the exact steps you took, and you'll be able to retrace your steps should something go awry.

The other thing about making mistakes is that they can also offer many personal insights. For instance, I am a huge procrastinator. I can leave anything until the last minute. Even if it is or ever will be the most important thing to happen in my life, I will still find a way to push it off until it's crunch time. I have, for the most part, come to accept this about myself. It feels like it's an attention thing, like when the pressure is on, I can finally focus, but without the pressure of a looming deadline, my mind just wanders like it's walking through a sunlit meadow. When it comes to my witchcraft practice, this means setting "deadlines" for my learning. I'll use my digital calendar to mark down the start date of when I begin reading a new book, and I'll log in an end date, the day that I am supposed to have it finished by. This reading deadline isn't enforced by anyone but myself, but it gives me that extra push I need because I also have a bad habit of getting a wandering eye when it comes to books.

In my spellwork this means that if I want to produce a result that I need immediately, it usually has a better outcome. This will not, I repeat, *not* be the same for everyone; all I know is that when I really need something by a certain date, all my energy goes toward getting it. That also includes the energy I put into the spell. I try not to worry about it that much anymore and use my habit of procrastination to my advantage. If we start to see our mistakes as airport traffic control signals, waving us along in the right direction, we can stop taking our mistakes to bed with us at night. We've all been awake at three a.m. thinking about something we did four years ago that we regret, and it feels gross.

I've made so many mistakes in my life that if I had a blooper reel, it would play without repeating for at least six years straight.

RECORDING YOUR SPELLS

First, don't let the lack of outcome or mistakes stop you from trying new spells. Too many witches stop themselves because of this, and it is a real shame because they are powerful witches and everyone starts somewhere. Everyone has spells that don't turn out right. When starting your next spell, write everything down, and I mean everything! The date, time, materials, etc. This will serve you well as you move forward. Having a record of everything you are doing makes it a whole lot easier to change things, and it gives you the chance to step back later and see things from a fresh perspective. Basically, record everything as if your spellwork depended on it, because if your spells aren't working right now, they just might.

Spell Record Keeping Checklist:
1. Record the date (month, day of the week)
2. Time of the spell
3. Moon phase
4. Materials you are using and amount of each ingredient (herbs, crystals, salts, alcohol, etc.)
5. The order in which you are adding them to the spell
6. The direction you were facing when conducting the spell
7. The way you conducted the spell (did you stir something clockwise, etc.)
8. How you closed the spell
9. Any actions you took immediately after the spell

Once you've recorded all of that and gone through the spell, now you must wait. While you're waiting, there are some variables to consider. Let's say you conducted a spell and within that spell you wrote a time limit of when you wanted the outcome by. For example, you were doing a spell to bring about three new tarot reading clients by the end of the month. If the end of the month passes and you had three new clients come to you, your spell worked, and you have a success. If the end of the month passes and you did not get the three clients you wanted, you know you have some tweaking to do.

You must go back to the drawing board. Look back at the record you wrote down. You have a fresh perspective now to see if anything was off. You may immediately recognize that you conducted the spell on a Tuesday and realize that Thursday is the day for abundance, so you should have conducted the spell on that day instead. There are methods to the madness! You can change, rearrange, and organize the spell as much as you want and then try again. I suggest leaving some room in between the spells— a little breathing room always feels good and seems to clear the energy for the second time around.

Allowing some time to pass will also let you analyze the actions you took after the spell was conducted. A spell is something that assists you in achieving that which you manifest, but you still have to put in the work to receive the desired outcome. Think of a spell like learning to ride a bike: the spell helps you in the beginning and gets you started, but it is you that must learn to peddle, stay balanced, and keep momentum. If you performed the spell for three tarot clients but did not follow through by promoting yourself and letting people know you were available for readings, then of course the spell didn't work! There needs to be both the magick and the effort.

When you *do* conduct a spell that works, make sure to take note. If it is a spell that asks for an outcome that can be replicated, like a spell for tarot clients, you can repeat the spell that worked in the exact same way and see if you get duplicate results. If positive results occur the second time around, then you know you have found a spellcasting method that works.

Through all of this, you must trust your own inner guidance system. I know I sound like a broken record! Intuition is important because although there are correspondences for days of the week, moon phases, tarot card meanings…sometimes you must put your own spin on things. Your intuition will guide you, and if you are ever unsure, you can cross-reference and double-check the correspondences.

A magickal record allows us the freedom to spill our thoughts onto the page, record our spells, dive into who we are, and begin to truly know ourselves. Magick is power, and power comes from knowing yourself.

Chapter 9
THE ART OF LANGUAGE

A few months ago, I was invited to be a guest on Devin Hunter's podcast, *Modern Witch*. Devin is also an occult and witchcraft author and one that I had looked up to for some time, so when I got the chance to talk to him, I was very excited. Talking to Devin felt like an hour of intense learning even though it was only a conversation. I listened to the words he spoke, how much he cared about magick, and how he personally practiced. The experience of being a guest on the show and talking to Devin was enlightening and left me with much to think about.

That evening after speaking with him, I contemplated the very energy of the words that were flowing between us. It seems I had been just on the brink of understanding the true power of language and symbolism. I still don't claim to understand fully, but the very act of simply speaking to Devin felt like it unlocked something for me in understanding the magick that language and communication holds.

We know that the tarot is composed of a set of symbols; these symbols can easily speak to our subconscious mind because that's exactly how our subconscious mind speaks to us. Our dreams are symbols, and the emotions we feel aid in our understanding of both our dreams and outer symbols like the tarot. These symbols must have an essence. Throughout many occult books you might find that certain words have been rearranged or certain letters have been taken out and a new one added. This creates a new word. It is difficult to explain something that has only been an impression upon the mind or spirit and does not have a word yet to express it. We begin to see the art and play of language! Still, every essence not yet expressed by language can still be revealed through the pages through tone, feeling, and energy.

Every practicing occultist knows that you cannot get from the page that which you do not try for yourself. It could become a staple in your mind, some piece of intellectual knowledge that you have acquired, but it is through the experience that you learn the essence of the words that you read *and* that you speak. "It's all in your mind!" Devin said during the podcast interview. The Devil card in the Rider-Waite-Smith tarot depicts the devil with two individuals who are loosely chained, an illusion to matter. What holds us to this place but our beliefs, and where do these beliefs come from but the very words that we use to communicate? Language is one layer of communication that has a very powerful hold on the way we operate. Our world is full of projections and gnosis, all things that other people have told us, and we go on believing them and not questioning it, but as occultists it should be our aim to experience things for ourselves—to know the essence of the language they speak.

Speaking things into existence is making something real outside of your own internal perception; you create something from your mind and place it in the outside world. The experiences someone has would only be their experiences, but then someone else jumps in and says, "That sounds like this!" And then the individual says, "Oh, it *must* be that!" Spoken language creates something apart from the symbolic language of the soul, but the words themselves are just vehicles for the thought form. Language can be played with; it is just a vehicle for thought, energy, and creation. If you can change the name of something, does it lose its value? Do people continue believing in it? All that we currently believe is held together by ways of communication and language; this is a barrier we must all cross. If not everything is yet in a word, then symbol and experience are the rulers of the language of spirit.

Finally, in an interview, David Shoemaker once said, "At later stages, still before Knowledge and Conversation, you get refinements to ritual and symbol ... What you're essentially doing, and the movement toward Knowledge and Conversation, is building your own religion. And you are the prophet; you are the high priest or priestess. The rituals and symbols, and ritual gestures, and forms of worship ultimately will be crafted in an entirely unique way just for you and your Angel. And that happens very, very organically."[18]

Bond to language if it suits you but know that there are words yet unexpressed in the human language and that you have the freedom to find your own path both inward and outward, all expressed through symbol, energy, ritual, and your own understanding of the language as it is presented to you. For what is *God* beyond the name?

When thinking of language, there are many different types: spoken word, written word, sign language, symbol, and so on. They all convey something to us; they all hold a certain energy. They are one of the vehicles for energy and communication.

---

18. TheHighersideChats, "Dr. David Shoemaker | Thelemic Magick, Aleister Crowley, & Finding Your True Will," December 31, 2014, The Higherside Chats, YouTube video, 1:13:47, https://www.youtube.com/watch?v=DaYI3cJlirY.

Underneath the surface, sometimes that energy is the same, even though words, symbols, letters can all be different. Also, the written word can bring about certain emotions, states of mind, and knowledge ... it is truly a form of deep expression, one that the conscious mind can comprehend. Symbols are also a language, one that the subconscious mind comprehends and tries to bring to the surface of the conscious mind. This is why the tarot is often seen as a tool that can speak to the conscious mind and imprint the knowledge that lies within the cards.

Moving beyond the title of the tarot cards and diving deep into what the symbolism is impressing onto the mind is a crucial step in understanding the way language works. We don't always have to go off the label; we can explore the essence of what is being presented to us for ourselves. For a moment, let's return to our metaphor of the cosmos. Within each of our own galaxies we have a solar system; this is represented to us when we see our birth chart. In our birth chart, we see all of the planets and their placements at the time of our birth. Each planet has a name that serves as a unique identifier, just as each star in the sky usually has a unique number or name identifier and a lowercase Greek letter: a (alpha), b (beta), y (gamma), and so on.

But, back to the idea that we are a reflection of the galaxy at the time of our birth. The planet names are Mercury, Venus, Earth, Mars, Jupiter, Saturn, Uranus, Neptune, and Pluto. (The demotion of Pluto as a planet is still debated, but usually if you get ahold of your birth chart, it will be there, so I have added it.) If we only know these planets by name and we don't allow ourselves to dive deeper, we will only know them by the combinations of letters displayed on the page. What is the essence of a planet? What makes it so? It is important to begin to see beyond the word and peer into the realm of energy. In astrology, each of the planets are said to hold a certain energy and meaning. Mars rules action and aggressive energy, Venus rules love and beauty, Mercury rules communication, Jupiter rules growth and expansion, Saturn rules structure and discipline, Uranus rules change and rebellion, Neptune rules dreams and intuition, and Pluto rules transformation and rebirth. The Sun rules the personality, the Moon rules the shadow, and the rising sign rules the persona.

Now, let's return to the tarot for a moment to explore the names in relation to the energy of the cards. What is interesting about both examples, the planets and stars and the cards, is that they each come with correspondences—this is the general consensus around what each of them are to mean and represent. The only way to move beyond the general consensus and to know for certain is to try it for ourselves. Even more fascinating is that each time we peer into a planet, a star, or a tarot card we might come up with something new. Does this mean that the entire meaning changes? I believe that when we look at these things, we are ultimately looking at ourselves, so naturally at different times new aspects of ourselves will emerge and they, too, can be integrated into the whole.

The seventy-eight cards of the tarot can be broken down into the twenty-two cards of the major arcana, with the minor arcana being separated into four suits: wands, coins, swords, cups. Different tarot decks can depict different images and symbols, and so depending on the tarot deck of choice, there may be a unique energy to the card itself beyond the name. For the sake of this section, I am going to refer to the imagery of the Thoth Tarot, as I feel it will more accurately describe the message. Let us look at one of my favorite cards, the Two of Coins, otherwise known as Change. You can find the image of the card by doing a quick online search for "Change card Thoth Tarot."

CHANGE

In the Thoth Tarot, the Two of Coins is called Change. The image on the card shows two circles, one above the other; one is white, and the other is black. Within the two circles there are two yin-yang symbols, and around both of the larger circles there is a snake shaped like the infinity symbol. If we were to just look at the word *change*, we might be limited to thinking of this card as meaning only change in whatever suits our minds at the time. If we explore the symbology and essence of the card behind the word, we begin to see that more exists. We begin to see that by the union of opposites, change is stability and stability is change. The universe is like the ouroboros—continuously circling back into itself. And from this we can move beyond the word *change* and into the essence of the card itself, into the energy of the word for which the written language was just a vehicle.

MAGICK IN SHAKESPEARE

Finally, someone who I believe appreciated the art of language was Shakespeare. I was lucky enough to purchase an old copy of *Tales from Shakespeare* by Charles and Mary Lamb for only a dollar from my local thrift store. My entire day was filled with ecstasy, and I began reading the stories, eager to find out what made Shakespeare one of the greats. One of my favorite stories is *A Midsummer Night's Dream*. Within each word there seems to be so much magick. If you were to read the story on the surface, it might appear to be just a tale of fiction, but within the essence of the words there is hidden the art of glamour, love, and protection magick. And we cannot deny that the words themselves are put together in a most delicious way. For example, it is written:

He found Titania giving orders to her fairies, how they were to employ themselves while she slept. "Some of you," said her majesty, "must kill the cankers in the musk-rose buds, and some wage war with the bats for their leathern wings, to make my small elves coats; and some of you keep watch that the clamorous owl, that nightly hoots, come not near me; but first sing me to sleep." Then they began to sing this song:—

> *You spotted snakes with double tongue,*
> *Thorny hedgehogs, be not seen;*
> *Newts and blind-worms do no wrong,*
> *Come not near our Fairy Queen.*
> *Philomel, with melody,*
> *Sing in your sweet lullaby,*
> *Lulla, lulla, lullaby; lulla, lulla, lullaby;*
> *Never harm, nor spell, nor charm*
> *Come our lovely lady nigh;*
> *So good night with lullaby.*[19]

Try to read the quote above first normally, then try to see what is beneath the surface. What is happening in the passage? Well, it looks like a spell. What energy is being offered here? It appears to be a protection spell. This might lead you to explore the whole story or other works by Shakespeare. If you do, try to read each story first normally, then try to explore each word and begin to ask yourself why each one was chosen to be where it is in the text. What does the story tell us on the surface, and what is hiding underneath? Often stories will have a main plot and a subplot. It

---

19. Charles Lamb and Mary Lamb, *Tales from Shakespeare*, by William Shakespeare, Series for the Young, vol. 7 (Leipzig: Bernhard Tauchnitz, 1863), 30.

is up to you to discover the deeper meaning in much of what you read. Try rearranging some letters, reading the words out loud, drawing some of the words out to create symbols, and so on.

Magick is just as much about communication as it is about anything else, like devotion or spellwork or confidence. When we can learn to understand our language and the language of energy more deeply, many new and wonderful things will be revealed to us.

Chapter 10
MAGICKAL LIVING: THINGS TO CONSIDER

As we grow older, it can feel like life either speeds up and becomes more chaotic, or it can slow down and become a little more peaceful. I'm not going to pretend like we all had great childhoods that didn't leave us with things we are still working through. When I think of magickal living, I think of living life in a way that is best for us, even if it goes against the status quo. Living our own kind of magick can be rebellious and healing. Magick, after all, is sovereignty.

When making magick your own, it comes down to not just practicing that magick but living it also. Too often we rush off to work without enjoying the drive or even stopping to look at how beautiful the world around us can be on its own. When was the last time you stopped to appreciate the night sky or look up at the stars to make a wish? Magickal living doesn't mean abandoning our responsibilities. It is all about finding your own unique rhythm and moving accordingly.

Living a magickal life for me right now means slowing things down and prioritizing what matters. The word *prioritizing* can sound stale, but with so much of life being heavy, I make it a priority to steal moments for myself, to do things I used to do when

I was younger. In the summer months, I still make wishes on dandelion fluff. I think that we have been practitioners of magick since we were young, and those wishes were some of the first spells we ever cast. I know I still have much work to do in order to produce an outcome for my wish, but the universe has heard me, and that's more than enough in that moment.

For this reason, I have included a journaling prompt for you to go through in your own time. This is meant to get you thinking about ways in which you can bring small joys into your life and be present while they are happening.

EXERCISE
CHECK-IN JOURNAL PROMPT

Complete these prompts when you have set time aside to really dive into them. Think about the questions, digest them, and then write down the answer. Allow your thoughts to move from one to the next; you may just be surprised where your mind takes you.

1. When was the last time that I did something just for myself?

2. What small joys did I love as a child? This could be blowing bubbles, looking at the clouds, or reading a book under a tree.

3. What small joys do I enjoy today? Can you think of any?

4. What is stopping me from enjoying more small moments in life?

5. What is one thing I can do this week that I've always wanted to do or that I have been waiting to do?

6. What have I been avoiding or putting off that sounds like a lot of fun?

7. What gets in the way of me doing more fun things with myself and for myself?

8. How can I prioritize myself and my joy more in my life?

* * *

The freest I have ever felt is in realizing that I am me, flaws and all. I know that's something you hear quite often. You're always told growing up, "Just be yourself." I always thought that was a silly thing to say because at the time I thought I had to "find" myself, and I was still searching. It wasn't until my late twenties that I finally realized what being yourself really meant. I am me, flaws and all, and that's all I can ever be. That's when I settled into myself like an old sweater and started to feel more comfortable. I realized that they were right all along—that true power does come from within even when it's a little bit messy.

WORKING THE MAGICK

Walking our own magickal path means coming to terms with ourselves and the messy bits. For me, I had to realize that I had a terrible cycle of self-sabotage. In this case, I am referring to a time when we are in control, when we know something is going to work out for us, and then we deliberately wreck it. There are things in our lives that we cannot control, and on some level, our magick is a way to fight against that, but what I'm talking about here is when we cast a spell and it starts to work and then we stop it from working ourselves.

Whenever something was going too well in my life, I would ruin it. Whenever I was set to reach a new milestone, I would bring the whole house of cards down around myself until there was nothing left. I saw this cycle play out with my spells too. Over and over again I would spend the time creating and carrying out a spellcasting. I would gather all the materials, write out my petition, and carry out the necessary procedures, but when the outcome started to come to fruition in my life, I would stop it, and I began to feel hopeless, as if I was destined to just repeat the cycle without ever breaking free.

I began to look at what I was doing wrong, and most of the time, I was conducting the spell, but I was neglecting the most crucial part, the *work*. It became clear that I was closing doors for myself because I wasn't making it easy for the Divine to bring those things that I was casting spells for into my life. I'm a firm believer that the spell works by bringing what you want to you, but you must position yourself in such a way that you will be able to receive it.

By following through on the little tasks after the spell has been conducted, you bring yourself one step closer to success. I'm not going to say I'm a professional; I still have moments when I realize I have somehow started to self-sabotage *again* and need to course correct. Something that has helped me a great deal has been to take the role of the observer. This doesn't mean just checking out and never addressing any real issues, instead it means not immediately feeling guilty and beginning to trash talk myself when I make a mistake, or even worse, when I knowingly sabotage something for myself. Becoming the observer can be a bit tricky at first because you separate yourself from the outcome of the situation.

You take a moment to look at the situation from a balanced view-point to see everything for what it truly is. For the time being, you observe and look at the actions that got you to the point of sab-otage. You are there to learn and understand and nothing more.

Admittedly, this method has taken me a few tries, and each time I still feel like I'm not exactly doing it right. I have found that each time I enter the role of the observer, I come into a deeper understanding of myself and my own actions. Each time I pin down more of the reason *why* I self-sabotage, and that leads me to knowing I don't really need to. It has brought me to know that a lot of what I allow to hold me back is fear in disguise. On the outside it looks like a big, scary monster, but on the inside it's just a ball of fear. After you've done your observing, you can return to the full range of emotions. Journaling is great, and I am a huge advocate for its benefits, but sometimes a nice long walk down a familiar path is what's needed, other times it's to sit on the couch with a box of chocolate and some tissues. Do whatever works for you at that moment.

Don't get me wrong, I do believe in discipline; the more you do something the better you'll become at it, or at least the more confident you'll be in your practice. When people preach disci-pline in relation to spiritual practices, I truly believe it is because they see a benefit and they want others to experience it for them-selves. It's true that protection magick works best when a person has been taking steps to protect themselves each day through small tasks. If someone were to send a harmful hex your way but you had been performing the LBRP each day along with pray-ing and wearing a talisman of protection, chances are you won't notice anything and it won't affect you too much. If on the other hand you didn't have that protection practice, the hex might start to show signs of working in your life, and then it would take a lot more time and energy to correct. The same could be said about our small daily practices like journaling, turning over a tarot card, prayer, or protection rituals. I do agree that discipline when wanting to achieve something within our practice is important, but again we don't need to beat ourselves up for not doing it either. Everything has its time and season, and we can sometimes have a way of making ourselves feel worse about things than we need to. If I miss a few days of protection, I simply pick up where I left off.

Another thing that I was grateful to hear along my journey was that our practice should fit into our lives, not the other way around. When I first started performing a kind of daily sun salutation, which comes with the requirement of doing it four times a day, I would get upset that I couldn't get it done right at sunrise or sunset or right smack-dab at twelve o'clock in the afternoon. This, too, was a learning experience, as that kind of schedule won't be sustainable for everyone. What we do in our practice must be tailored to how we as individuals live or we will never stick with it long-term. This is how we make daily practice manageable: finding a way to take what we learn and make it fit us instead of trying to fit what everyone else is doing. There is no way I am going to be able to wake up at sunrise every day. I mean I could, but I'm just not going to, and I know that about myself, so I now perform Liber Resh whenever I wake up, and it has become a lot easier and less frustrating.

THE POWER OF DREAMS

Dreams are a part of daily practice for most people without them realizing it. Keeping a journal specifically for dreams is often something witches will do, or as spoken about in the magickal record keeping chapter, you can record them in your daily record.

I have had many dreams that stuck with me during the day, and after analyzing them, they have always pointed me toward something I was questioning or brought me to a more secure place on my path. Dreams are fascinating, and I like to think of them as being the hidden part of ourselves trying to communicate with us in the best way it knows how.

I have had many significant dreams. One of them was while I was working in an office with an office manager who wasn't very nice. Although she was nice to my face, she always found ways to get me in trouble with our boss, and I was always trying to defend myself against her attacks. A month before her sneaky games started, I had a dream about two foxes, and I awoke from that dream feeling a sense of unease. I didn't recognize it at the time, but I feel my dream was trying to warn me about the situation at hand. I ultimately ended up leaving that position, and although I don't regret my choice to leave, I do regret not seeing it sooner and possibly being able to counteract it. If I had taken the time to truly analyze my dream, I may have been more aware.

Another dream I had was when I had run into a tricky situation, and I was feeling a little powerless. I wasn't sure what to do, and so that night before going to bed I prayed for a sign. I slept through the whole night only to awake without having had a dream. That morning after getting a cup of tea, I sat back down in bed and began reading a book, only I felt so tired it was as if the moment I fell back asleep I was transported to another place. The sky above me was gray, and the clouds moved faster and faster— so fast, in fact, I began to get a little frightened. I then looked down at the ground, and it was covered in mist. As I looked back up, a large black dog started running after me, and that is when I woke up. I must have only been asleep for a few moments, but

I had my sign and my answer. I thought it meant to up my protection work, and so I did. I cast protection spells and did my protection magick twice daily. I even cleansed my home several times and began carrying with me extra talismans of protection.

Finally, one of my most significant dreams was the night my grandmother died. I was forty minutes away and asleep, but that night I had a dream that I was driving to my grandmother's house because something was wrong. As I got to the front door, she opened it and smiled; she was standing there looking so healthy, just the way she had looked before she got sick. She told me she was okay and that she loved me, and in my dream, I felt a great sense of relief. The next morning, my mother called me to tell me that my grandmother had passed away. To this day, I believe it was my grandmother telling me that she was okay and that she was in a better place with no more pain; it was her way of saying goodbye even while we were miles apart.

If nothing else, beginning to document your dreams is a great place to start in terms of having daily practice. Some days there won't be any dreams; other days there will be dreams that are pregnant with symbolism. I used to rush to look up a dream's meaning online, but I quickly came to find that no one will have a more accurate take on your dream than you, because it's your subconscious speaking to you. It's my advice that you spend the time to really digest the symbols that appear in your dreams, come to know how you feel about them, and begin to look at any factors currently going on in your life to which they might be speaking. Dreams are a gateway to understanding yourself, your will, and your path to the fullest.

COMMUNITY VS. SOLITARY

Many practitioners will have another choice to make: whether they want to practice in a community, order, or coven, or whether they would like to be more solitary. There are pros and cons to both. When looking to join a community of practitioners, it is okay to "shop around" in order to find the one that fits you best. So often, people think that they need to stick with the first community or coven that welcomes them, and although choosing and sticking to a dedicated path is beneficial for spiritual growth, it's important to ensure that your community fits with your own values on such a personal journey. Orders and covens can be beneficial for feeling connected and having other people who are on a similar path to yours. They also largely serve as educational tools with mentorship to help teach and guide a person on their path.

The truth is that the more people you are around, the more groups form, there will be people you run into that you just don't get along with. Whenever there are larger groups of people, there will be those with big egos, those who want to control, or those who have some sort of emotional outburst. If we are completely honest with ourselves, we have all found ourselves on both sides of the spectrum in different situations. That being said, you should always have your own values and boundaries set before entering into a community. My own practice greatly improved once I was able to learn from others in a more structured way, but everyone is different, so you must at all costs find what works for you.

There's also the decision to be a solitary practitioner. This path is for those who may not have the opportunity to be in an area where there are covens or orders, or for those who simply feel best when they walk a completely individual path. For solitary practitioners, they may also find a sense of belonging in the wider online occult community by attending events and workshops, building friendships, or being a part of an occult book club. Solitary practitioners may be those who follow a set path or system of magick, or they may feel inclined to create their own. Whether you choose to be part of a community, large or small, or whether you choose to practice in a solitary manner, you can still find connection on your journey through the relationships you foster.

MAKING MONEY FROM YOUR MAGICK

Finally, the last topic I wanted to touch on when living a magickal life is the choice of whether or not to make money from your magick. There has also been debate on whether this is right or wrong. My understanding of it is that if you enter into a magickal order you will swear not to reveal certain carefully guarded secrets. If you don't reveal the secrets, then surely you can write books or sling cards or do anything you like. I myself have been hit with both sides of the debate. My great-grandmother believed that you shouldn't charge for a tarot reading and that it should be given freely, as the tarot is a powerful tool of divination and self-exploration. Of course, I have charged for tarot readings and found that I was spending significant time and energy to give them, so accepting payment wasn't an issue. Of course, when it comes to teaching magick, we need to be sure that we trust those who are educating us and that their intentions are pure. When it comes to money, sometimes it gets in the way of people's judgments and motives. It is important to always maintain integrity if you are choosing to make money from your magick and to be careful who we choose to learn from.

That being said, making money from your magick can look like having a business where you give readings, offer spellwork, or create and sell occult tools. It can also look like spells conducted in order to bring in money. In the occult community the usual argument for not making money with your magick is that you are not supposed to share the secrets of an order you are in. That is understandable; if you join a secret society and you take an oath, then don't write a book and spill all the secrets. But that doesn't mean that you can't still write books, teach classes, or give lectures. I see every book, class, and lecture as a stepping-stone that allows me to learn more about magick and myself. If there are any secrets to learn, I'll learn them by doing the work.

Regardless, making money from your magick is a personal choice and one that I don't believe should be shamed. There are so many people making money in areas that they don't care about at all; this makes those spaces very toxic. Shouldn't we want people to make money in the area of magick and witchcraft who actually enjoy it, who are passionate about it, and who actually live their magick every single day? If you choose to make money from your magick, it is my belief that you should do so unapologetically because there will always be someone out there who tries to stop you or tries to tell you that you are wrong for doing so. But you have your own path, and if you are genuine in what you do and you know it is the right thing for you, then do it and don't let anyone stop you. Those who choose to not make money from their magick are not any better nor any worse than those who do.

If you choose to, there may be other things to consider like burnout and making sure that you continue to maintain your own personal practice. Sometimes when we do something for work, we find ourselves taking breaks from it when we are not working. I have always thought this to be the biggest commitment those who work with their magick make; it takes time and energy, along with a high level of emotional intelligence and customer service skills. It takes creating a strong working relationship with the deities you connect with and setting strong boundaries between work and life. Finding ways to return to your personal practice and making sure that you set aside time for yourself will be crucial for the longevity of your work and spiritual path. It is a very personal decision either way and one that I don't think many practitioners take lightly.

Chapter 11
DIGITAL MAGICK

Digital magick is something that is quickly progressing, especially now that we have the birth of Web 3.0, which many see as the next evolution of the internet. Although, there are debates about Web 2.0 and Web 3.0 being developed parallel to each other, where individuals can choose which to participate in.

I have come across some people who suggest that magick and technology do not mix and that it would be best to keep them separate, but I think they are inherently linked. If magick is causing change in conformity with will, then technology is surely a by-product of someone's magick.[20] If you look for both the good and the bad, you will find that technology has hurt our lives and helped our lives in many ways. We are more connected than ever, yet more and more people report feeling lonely and isolated. Advancements in technology help doctors and surgeons work better, help people who wouldn't otherwise be able to have access to education or employment do so remotely, and allows for families to stay in touch from miles apart.

---

20. Aleister Crowley, *Magick in Theory and Practice* (New York: Dover Publications, 1929), xii.

When I was growing up, I wasn't allowed to have a phone until I turned fourteen, and when I got it, it was a big red brick phone that was indestructible. It had no social media apps, no FaceTime, no camera. It was all about the text message, and you had to pay for each one you sent. When we got our first family computer, we didn't have Wi-Fi; we used the phone jack, and if you were on the internet, the landline wouldn't work. When the computer would turn on and begin connecting to the internet it would make loud screeching noises. It sounds weird to say now, but it's true! The birth of the internet literally screamed at us.

Now, of course, we have social media, video conferencing, VR/AR, and so much more. At the time of writing this, we have moved into exciting waters that look eerily familiar to the '90s and the dotcom craze. The buzzword on the street is blockchain technology, and everyone thinks it's going to change the way the online world works and allow for creators to have ownership over their intellectual and digital property and data. Now more than ever we are at a new frontier, and magick has a place in where we are going. Over the past few years, I have begun to mix more magick into the way I use technology, and if I'm being completely honest these days, I'm on it all the time. I'm either creating something with my laptop or surfing social media on my phone. I used to bring my phone with me when I went for walks in the woods so that I could take pictures, but I decided to leave it behind most days now and just be present and enjoy nature without needing to capture it. I think technology is a powerful tool, but we all need to take breaks every now and then.

In this chapter, I hope to get you thinking about different ways that magick and technology can come together. Technology is another tool at our fingertips that we can use to bring our will into the world. It offers us a chance to socialize with people all over the world, build community, command influence, and access great power. Technology can help to spread awareness and ideas and to create change—it is all in how we use it.

TECHNOLOGY AND OWNERSHIP

When the internet first started, it was just text on a screen. Then it moved to social apps where people could create content like blogs, videos, and photos and share them with people. Unfortunately, what happened was the platforms owned the content and the creators were left essentially borrowing the apps' features. Now, people are working on a different future, one that will allow creators to own what they create and what they earn.

Digital Identity

Today, everyone will search for you online; whether it is someone you meet at a coffee shop or a potential employer, they will probably ask for a link to your social profiles or online resume. This is a digital reputation. Everything you put online crafts an image, and it is you who is in charge of that image.

In the book *The 48 Laws of Power* by Robert Greene, the chapter dedicated to the fifth law is titled "So much depends on reputation—guard it with your life."[21] Reputation is like an egregore; it is something that you can build upon, and it will live on long after you are gone. A digital identity has the potential to place you in front of new people every day, and it can gift you great opportunities. Everyone will have a different digital identity, and we see this today in a variety of professions. There are people who are known for being funny, serious, quirky, bookish. We see a new crop of

---

21. Robert Greene, *The 48 Laws of Power* (London: Profile Books, 2000), 37.

titles being used by people such as "thought leader" and "futurist." You can arguably choose what you would like to be known for and work toward that through skill, effort, time, and your reputation, which is largely digital. We now even have robot influencers who have teams of people working behind the scenes. These robot influencers have worked with large brands much in the same way a human influencer would. In the future we will see that all of the platforms we use, the blogs we create, the things we do will be tied to one digital identity. It will be a very powerful thing.

DIGITAL EGREGORES

An egregore is a thought-form created through a collective energy. A group of people focusing on the same topic feeds an energy into the topic or idea, and it takes on a life of its own. The example that I always go to is that of Terence McKenna. He was an ethnobotanist and philosopher who advocated for the use of psychedelic substances. He had a brilliant mind, and many of his lectures can still be found online today. This means that his energy has lived on without him and continues to change individual lives every single day by opening their minds to new ideas and concepts of thought. Just like McKenna, we, too, can create a digital egregore by creating and publishing content online. When we post our art, thoughts, ideas, values, spiritual beliefs, etc., it creates an image around us; it creates our digital reputation. This reputation is then seen by lots of people and has the potential to live on as an egregore.

Take money, for example: for most people it is an egregore. We as humans think about it all the time, work toward it, and give our energy to it, and it becomes this collective energy that has value because we give it value. Now, money is going even more digital and has the potential to soon become completely digital. Money is one form of digital egregore.

Brands are also a form of egregore. When we think of a brand we like, it provokes a certain emotion and energy from us. Sometimes we even love brands without knowing why we love them. This could be due to intelligent and slick marketing (and most likely is) or any number of other things like color psychology, logo design, mission statement, and so on. When enough people jump on board and start loving a brand, it starts to live in group thought and become a thought-form of its own. We live in a time when brands go digital to get exposure because that is where all the attention is. Brands are a form of digital egregore. We see brands and corporations following the attention once again by launching themselves into the metaverse. J. P. Morgan, Nike, Adidas, Louis Vuitton, and more have all begun to make their own metaverse locations as well as bring their products into the space.

EXERCISE
CREATING A DIGITAL EGREGORE

There may be times in your life when you want to create a digital egregore, a curated energy in the online world. We are all so multifaceted, and sometimes parts of our identity are better suited for digital egregores, while others find peace alone while reading or creating without showing those creations to the world. It is okay to be both. Should you want to create a digital egregore in order to find employment, put your work out there, join a community, or for some other reason, these steps may help you.

You will need:

- Laptop or phone

The steps:

1. The first step in creating a digital egregore is to think about the image you are creating, or the product, idea, or creation you are wanting to build. This will be different for everyone depending on your goals and motivations. For example, if you are a huge movie lover and you want to create a blog for movie reviews, you'll be creating a digital image and brand that represents your love of movies.

2. The next step is to think about how best you communicate. Some people are really great at video; they seem to come alive in front of the camera. Others may communicate best with audio or written word, and others still might use photos. It is okay to choose more than one, but try to really think about how best you communicate and what feels most natural to you.

3. Next, you'll want to start putting stuff out there! Perhaps you choose one social platform that you love or start a blog. If you are trying to grow a portfolio to gain employment, you might use a more professional platform and start writing or creating videos that show your expertise. Remember, this is about you having control over what you share with the outside world.

4. Finally, keep going and tailor as needed. Many people create digital egregores when they put their

small business online; they just don't call it that. You are building something that will capture attention and be viewed by people even while you are not directly operating it. You are in control of the energy, the words, the art, etc.

5. The more people that focus their energy on it along with you, the more success you may have. This isn't about being fake, but it is about understanding the great power that technology holds to get an idea off the ground or to start something new.

Technology can be used for good, which is why every day people are gifted with opportunities to work at their dream job simply because they began sharing what they love online. If you have a particular hobby, passion, or career field you would like to share, you might think about creating a digital egregore!

* * *

While practicing the above exercise and creating a digital egregore you can also help it along by feeding energy into it through journaling or meditating. Focus on what outcome you are wanting for your digital egregore. It could be to create a community around a hobby, land your dream job by building a digital portfolio, or simply engage with others who have similar interests. Whatever your goal, there's no harm in setting aside time each week to consciously focus on it or write a few journal pages about it. This will allow you to carve out a clear direction forward.

Now that we've covered egregores, the next logical step is to talk about creating and utilizing digital servitors—the next best thing!

DIGITAL SERVITORS

Servitors are one of my favorite ways to practice magick because they can be customized, created, and deconstructed, and they can serve a whole host of different purposes. The biggest reason why I love servitors is because they don't take any extra materials to make; if you have yourself, that's enough. It is important to keep in mind that everything is customizable and that you can use whatever you have accessible to you in the moment. No servitor is any more or less powerful based on the tools used.

Before we dive in headfirst, let's go over a few things that might be important. First, what is a servitor? According to Phil Hine, "A servitor is an entity consciously created or generated, using evocatory techniques, to perform a task or service."[22] This servitor is programmed to carry out specific tasks for you and assist you in obtaining the outcome(s) you desire. Next, we must learn how to make a servitor, and then we can talk about all the customizations.

When it comes to creating a digital servitor, this is a servitor that will live in a digital home on your desktop, phone, or in a game, and it will assist you with some kind of magick where technology is involved. It could help you land a job when you are sending out resumes through email, help you with networking online, help to grow your social media to sell your art, and so on.

EXERCISE
CREATING A DIGITAL SERVITOR

A digital servitor is an energetic form that has a set purpose and mission. You create the servitor and program

---

22. Phil Hine, *Condensed Chaos: An Introduction to Chaos Magic* (Tempe, AZ: The Original Falcon Press, 1995), 105.

it to complete its mission for you. Instead of it being a collective energy like the egregore, it is created from your individual energy.

You will need:

- Pen and paper, or laptop to use as a notepad
- Phone, laptop, or other digital item for housing your servitor once we get to the file housing exercise

The steps:

1. The first step in creating a servitor is to decide whether you would like to create it for one specific task or if it will be used for numerous tasks. The decision itself won't change much for the making and programing of the servitor, but once the servitor has fulfilled its first task, you can choose to either disassemble it or reprogram it for a different purpose.

2. Next, you will have to narrow down your first *specific intention*. About specific intentions, Phil Hine writes, "Here, you are creating the core of the Servitor's purpose—the Statement of Intent which is analogous to the Servitor's aetheric DNA."[23] Some of the reasons I have used a servitor in my life were to assist in gaining employment, help sell my first book, and successfully complete a course with subject matter that I was struggling with at the time. With each of these scenarios, I found myself feeling like I just needed some help, and by using a little magick, I was able to help myself succeed.

---

23. Hine, *Condensed Chaos*, 106.

3. Once you have chosen a specific intention or reason for creating the servitor, now it is time to move into visualization and programming. I have always felt that to program the servitor I needed to have its visuals mapped out first and really see it before me, either in my mind's eye or in another form like a drawing. Or, in this case, digitally on the computer or as a character in a game. For this phase of servitor creation, you'll need to think of what your servitor will look like. It could look like anything you want; this is the time to use your imagination. Once you've decided on what you want it to look like, really take the time to visualize it in your mind and make it real for you; after that you can begin to program it.

4. To program the servitor, you will need to be very specific about what you are wanting it to do. By now you have the general intention, but now it's time to get very detailed. Here are the questions you need to answer:

   - What is this servitor's specific task(s)?
   - How will it carry them out?
   - Will it have free reign to carry out these tasks as it sees fit or in a way you have specified?
   - How will the servitor be charged? (Thinking about it, through sigils, activities like lighting candles, etc.)
   - What is the time limit on carrying out the tasks?
   - When the task has been completed, what will it look like? How will it have impacted your life?

- How will the servitor be dissipated? Will it vanish after it has completed the task, or will it vanish after you have said a special word?

5. All of these are important because they will shape what the servitor does and how it goes about its work. After you have taken the time to get specific and know what you want the servitor to do, you can then instruct the servitor by visualizing it, reading the list aloud, and saying something like, "I activate you to carry out these tasks in this way and this way only," proceeding to read the list. If you have set a time limit for your servitor, you can then read out loud the time limit, saying something like, "You have exactly thirty days to carry out this task, once the task is completed, you will dissipate and be inactive."

You have now created the digital servitor, and it is time to give it a home, somewhere it will stay for the duration of its working.

* * *

EXERCISE
FILE HOUSING FOR DIGITAL SERVITOR

A home for your servitor could be in a digital file on your computer, a private social media profile, downloaded onto a hard drive, or as a character in a certain video game. (If you go the video game route, I do suggest choosing a game with a similar energy to what you are wanting the servitor to do.) Now that we have the creation of characters using programs like Unreal Engine that will be able to live in the metaverse, this is also an option as we move into the future.

You will need:

- Digital medium of your choice

The steps:

1. Create a new file on your desktop.

2. Find or create an image of what you want the servitor to look like.

3. Decide on the intent of your servitor and what you would like it to do.

4. Type up the servitor's instructions on a Word document, be very specific about what you would like it to do, its lifespan, etc.

5. Place both the image and the instructions into the new file you have created.

6. Create a sigil or find other images of correspondences that you can include in the file. This could also be poetry, lists of words, etc.

7. Focus your energy on the file and visualizing the servitor, and activate it by the method mentioned above.

8. Keep the file on your desktop until the task has been completed. When finished, simply delete the file.

* * *

The servitor that you have created can be reprogrammed for use on multiple projects if you like. In order to do this, I usually wait until I am sure the first task has been carried out completely. Then I will absolve the servitor of its original task by cleansing the space and deleting the original housing file from my computer. Once I have done this, I then follow the creation and programming steps again with the same servitor in mind.

EXERCISE
CREATING A MONEY SERVITOR

Now I will take you through the process of creating a digital servitor for bringing in money. I believe money to be an egregore, and it is an energy that we can turn into a servitor, something that will work for us. Here is my way of doing it.

You will need:
- Your online banking on your computer or phone
- Photos saved onto your computer or phone of things that symbolize money coming your way, like paid bills, photos of the things you want to do with money, etc.
- A digital file created to house your servitor and the corresponding photos

The steps:
1. On your altar, open your phone or computer and go to your banking app.
2. On the screen, draw an invoking pentagram. With your finger or wand, start from the top of the

pentagram, going down the left side, and follow through with tracing the rest of the pentagram.

3. Once the pentagram has been traced, begin to think about what you want your servitor to look like. This will serve you as you move forward because we will be drawing down energy from the egregore, and it is much easier to bottle something when you know where it is going.

4. Now, begin to think about what you want the servitor of money to do for you. This can be very specific things like pay the bills on time, find more opportunity, or help you get a raise, but it could also include some generalizations like helping you to feel more confident in your ability to manage your finances.

5. Now that you are ready with your visual of the servitor and you have narrowed down what it will do, you can begin to draw energy from the egregore of money and bottle it into your servitor. Take a moment to imagine the great big egregore of money with all its collective energy and all of the time people spend thinking about it, talking about it, and doing things to get it. Then, imagine it to be like a big ball of color, any color you like—most people might go for green. When you are ready, imagine pulling down some of that energy, and as you do, a smaller ball of color forms. Take this, and in your mind, very strongly place it into the servitor you have created. Imagine that this ball of color now fills your entire servitor.

6. Now, speak it into existence, saying, "You are now the servitor of money; you shall assist me with my tasks and bring me comfort, security, and opportunity." Then, program your servitor by reading out loud the instructions you have set.

7. Once you have finished programming it, set the servitor up in its home by visualizing it entering the digital file and place all of the photos you have collected into the file also. If you have programmed it to receive more energy every time someone thinks of money, then surely your servitor will be fed and working for you for life.

* * *

DIGITAL MONEY MAGICK

Another way of digitally working money magick is to focus on where the money goes and where it is held for you. This can be done through meditation and visualization, and there need not be any way of knowing *how* the spell will get accomplished, only the belief that it will be. For example, my partner once told me of a meditation they did to bring money in, and within the next few days, they received one hundred dollars. Now, you may be thinking one hundred dollars isn't a lot, but to some people it is!

EXERCISE
MONEY VISUALIZATION

This is a powerful meditation that requires a lot of energy. When we focus on bringing something to us, it can require a lot from us; we must believe in the magick, and we must know that what we desire is on its way. The time and energy we spend visualizing the outcome *is* magick because we are focusing our intent and will in order to create change.

You will need:

- Your bank account open on your phone, computer, or wherever you can see it

The steps:

1. Find yourself in a comfortable spot where you'll be able to focus for an extended amount of time. What I have found best, especially for those with attention problems like myself, is to do this meditation potently for two to five minutes at a time. Focus, then take a break and come back to it. It can be hard to stay focused on something like this for ten to twenty minutes or longer, so if you can't, that's okay; accumulated focus over time will work.

2. When you are ready, open your banking app so you can see your bank account. It doesn't matter what is in there right now; all that matters is what is coming to you through your magick.

3. Begin to look at the number and start drawing on the screen what you want the number to be. Maybe you need to add more zeros, or maybe you want a whole new number—whatever it is, continue to draw it on the screen. Keep repeating this over and over and over again.

4. As you trace the number on the screen, focus your intention on calling it to you; feel the feeling of having that money in the account.

5. Continue to do this until you feel it is done, and then you can say, "That amount is coming to me now, so shall it be."

You may feel tired after this exercise, and I suggest resting or replenishing in some way through food or drink. Over the next few days and weeks, it is important to remember that magick works in many ways, so there may be opportunities presented to you that you may need to take action on in order to get the money you have just summoned.

A few months ago, my partner and I went out under a full moon in the dark to conduct a spell to help with a school program; later that week, my partner was gifted with a computer. "That was fast … and a little easy," I thought, but the truth is my partner still has to do the work or else now we just have a computer. Don't be surprised if things start to happen, but remember that it will still take some effort on your part.

* * *

DIGITAL PROTECTION

As you spend time on social media, in the metaverse, or surfing the internet, you might need some protection. We will cover the basics and some extra measures you can take to protect yourself and your energy.

Staying safe in the digital world is important, and I stand by not sharing your address or too much personal information. In a previous chapter, we spoke about the debate of whether or not to share photos of your altar online; this same debate happens when people talk about sharing birth charts or other information about the practitioner themselves. It is true that anything you share about yourself could be used by another to cast magick upon you, and yes, we must guard against this, but most of what we share online these days will be personal to some extent or another.

If you keep up with daily protection work, then in most cases you will be fine. Remember that you can cleanse your own aura at any time after spending time online. Sometimes this is needed, and for those who are more sensitive to the energies around them, they may find themselves becoming drained by being on different social platforms or spending too much time online. This is because you are tapping into the collective consciousness that is the digital mind. It is the collection of everyone's thoughts, feelings, and creations uploaded into the cosmos of the digital plane. When you plug into it, you aren't just plugging into your own energy; you're plugging into the whole collective. Of course, the very practical reason for not divulging all of your information online is to keep you physically safe as well. Don't post your address, watch who you share personal information with, protect yourself, and be smart about who you interact with. If your intuition tells you something is off, listen to it.

Another method could be to protect your energy with an apps filter. This is a form of digital glamour magick, as you are concealing something, either your physical appearance or your energy, from the general public. Filters are great because they allow you to experiment and create with freedom all while keeping a digital layer of protection. Glamour magick can prove to be a great friend to the practicing magician who wants to keep some privacy in their lives, especially when operating in online spaces.

Digital magick is endless, and if you find yourself venturing down the rabbit hole, you will see it can be combined with many forms of magick, such as ceremonial or chaos magick. As was stated in the magickal record keeping chapter, you can keep a digital magickal record and use spreadsheets and graphs to see if there are any patterns in your practice. Today, technology is more a part of people's practices than we would like to admit. Digital magick alone offers a fascinating world of creation and mystery. You can create new things and send your ideas into the world. If you choose to explore digital magick further, I hope you find it as fulfilling as I do.

Chapter 12
CONFRONTING YOUR OWN PROGRAMMING

There are many ways that one can confront their own programming. I will be talking about it in the sense that an individual can get stuck in certain cycles of habit or thought and by taking certain steps might be able to break up their own perception. This may help to carry out healthier habits, actions, and thoughts, or those more in alignment with their true nature.

This is especially helpful when an individual cannot see the whole galaxy, or larger picture, and they believe themselves to only be one small part of it, one small star or planet. I'm not saying you must believe you literally are the entire universe, but it is metaphorically reflected within you. For example, it is common practice amongst many to look at their horoscope by only the Sun sign. This could be helpful to some extent, but it would be far more accurate to look at the whole and see that all planets are within your own galaxy and that one planet or one giant star (the Sun) is not all that you are. Perhaps you even extend beyond the parameters of this galaxy—perhaps you are ever expanding until the point of dissolution.

It is necessary at times to get a bigger picture, to look objectively at your own programming in order to see the best way forward. There is not just one way to confront your own programming but multiple ways, and far more than I myself know of. I will try my best to explain the ways that I have personally explored; beyond that, it will be up to you to find new ways of viewing yourself from new perspectives.

In the computer world, there is something known as *metaprogramming*. Metaprogramming is when code can write code itself. The programmer writes an initial code that allows the code to analyze itself and make adjustments. This means that we need data, the code, and an initial outside programmer.

Data = numbers and symbols (nouns). Code = data formulated to take action (verbs). In metaprogramming, we can write programs that themselves write programs.

With this theory applied to magick, we might think that a system of magick acts like a program and that the individual is a part of the code with its own unique data. When an individual begins upon a system of magick, it gives them the ability to analyze themselves, which provides more data, and from the data presented they can further program themselves. What data might an individual be able to bring to the program?

The data an individual has initially will be their birth chart. From this we have the time of birth, date, location, and astrological placements. This data can then be analyzed, and more data can be extracted from it. As one continues to write a detailed journal or magickal record, the "code," or individual, can analyze themselves, presenting more data and allowing for the emergence of patterns. Now, we might be concerned that the very nature of the journal will be biased because it is only coming from the perspective of the individual. This can be tricky because if the only data the code has to go off of is itself, how will it know if it is on the right path? Here is where a blend of intuition and communication with a higher source comes into play: the programmer itself. The programmer could be an entirely outside source, a creator that has started everything and set it all in motion, or it could be a part of the self that has yet to be realized operating from an outside dimension. Either way, the best policy is to let the magician come to an understanding of what they believe the programmer to be.

All of this does suggest that we need an unbiased way of extracting and viewing data. This could be done through peer review, and a mentor in a system of magick may be able to guide the way, especially if they have already gone down the path themselves. It could also be done by having an outside source as an identity marker for the individual. For example, it is much easier to see how fast a plane is moving when there are clouds in the sky. Without the clouds, there is nothing to compare its speed against. With the idea of confronting our own programming, one might come to the conclusion that we, too, need a point of reference.

Truth, for example, is sometimes thought of as what one *believes* to be true. In order to know it is indeed true, it must be verified. The same is true internally: our conscious mind is but an illusion because something else is perceiving it. In order to find an ultimate truth, we need unbiased data and unbiased analysis or analysis from an outside source (the programmer).

Coming to unbiased data as a human is very difficult because everything humans perceive is through their own mind; the truest form of data would then be that which is perceived from a place of equilibrium. Equilibrium is the desired starting point, and therefore any action before reaching that state is only to get there.

UNBIASED DATA BEFORE EQUILIBRIUM

Before equilibrium is achieved in the individual, one must still use the data provided to analyze oneself to the best of their ability. By looking at the data, we will be biased from the beginning. We can also seek the insight of someone outside of ourselves who is skilled in reading the data. Our magickal journals can also be seen as data pools where we can extract data and then "rewrite the code." We must have courage to look at all parts of ourselves, for if we cling to one side or the other, we cannot and will not come to know true equilibrium. When analyzing our own data from our journals, it is best to not search for one outcome over the other but to remain unbiased in search of the truth that reveals itself on the page.

All of this begs the question, can the program come into contact with the programmer? It would be one thing if the original programmer wrote the code and then retired, leaving it to write itself. This could bring about many problems if the code did not realize that it was also part of the programmer. If we think of a program as a walled garden, then it would need outside information in order to function properly. In ceremonial magick, we might think of the Holy Guardian Angel (HGA) as the thing that feeds information into the program (individual). Does this mean that the HGA also gets its information from an outside source or that it is the source itself? I don't have the answer, but it is an interesting question to ask.

It could be that the Holy Guardian Angel, the godhead, or the gods themselves are both internal and external, and therefore it is getting information from an "external source" and feeding it into the internal program. It may be possible if the HGA existed throughout multiple dimensions simultaneously, as lower dimensions would not be able to perceive the higher dimensions and it would therefore be unknown to the program (or individual) that the HGA was indeed part of themselves while also extending across time and space.

However you choose to confront your own programming, it will not be an easy feat. It is a challenging process, one that often happens over many years.

SHADOW WORK

Shadow work is itself a kind of metaprogramming because the act is like adaptive self-reflection. Seeing as the shadow is repressed, our conscious mind does not know what it is and does not perceive it, which means we are only given clues as to what lives in the depths of ourselves. These clues can come out in our magickal journal and throughout our daily lives. It can feel like an emotional trigger, something that pulls at us or something that we immediately turn from. Strong emotions toward something are often an indication of a shadow element at play.

The act of doing shadow work doesn't happen in one go, and it is never a process that is totally finished. As long as a human goes on living and interacting and engaging with the world around them, there will always be a shadow. It is best to enter into the idea without the thought of reaching a final destination, but as something that you can be aware of throughout your journey. A magickal record or journal allows for you to write down your reflections, thoughts, insights, gnosis, etc. Throughout the pages you will begin to see parts of yourself that make you question your own habits and motives, and when a part of the shadow comes to the surface, you will eventually need to deal with it. When something comes out of the shadow, it cannot become repressed again;

it has been brought forth from the subconscious mind into the conscious mind and will linger there until fully integrated.

The shadow can sometimes be sneaky. One example might be a parent who doesn't believe themselves to be a "helicopter parent." They might say, "I am not a helicopter parent; I just like to know what my children are doing at all times so that I can help them whenever they need." That sentence doesn't have anything wrong with it; surely a good parent is going to know what their children are up to and accommodate their needs! But let's say this particular parent has the pattern of routinely breaking their child's trust by rifling through their personal diary, giving them no privacy, and not allowing the child to fail at anything. This could be harmful to the child in the long run, and surely the child would find ways to hide things from the parent out of sheer desire to have something for their own! The parent denies being a "helicopter parent" and refuses to inspect the idea to see if there is a kernel of truth. This would be a repressed shadow yet to be recognized.

Upon the recognition of a shadow, there are some decisions to make! Does the individual further deny it? Perhaps their ego is trying to save them some tough feelings by turning the other way. Do they accept the truth of the shadow? Do they do any further work to dig deeper into why this shadow exists and what might be done about it? This is the *work* part of shadow work. As you can see, it can assist someone in confronting their own programming if they were so inclined to begin the process of thorough self-examination through courage!

ALTERED STATES OF CONSCIOUSNESS

Entering into an altered state of consciousness is another way of confronting your own programming, getting to see it from a different perspective. Drugs are not the only way to change your perspective, and altered states of consciousness can happen through meditation, breathwork, exercise, sex, etc. They are when we peer into the habits we've been keeping and see room for any adjustments. I cannot speak to many other forms, so I will say the methods that have worked for me so far have been by way of cannabis, sex, and physical exercise. Through these three methods, I have been able to open my mind to new possibilities, new gnosis, and new ways of thinking about my galaxy and its role in the universe.

My own experience, and one that left an impact on my life after I regained full sobriety, was with smoking cannabis in a controlled setting. I hadn't smoked cannabis for many years but thought that I might give it a try and see if it shook anything up. I sat on my bed with my back against the wall. Before smoking, I said out loud, "Angel, tell me what I need to know." I thought that by entering into an altered state of consciousness I might be able to receive the Knowledge and Conversation of the Holy Guardian Angel that I had been chasing. At first it started off fine; I felt very relaxed, and it felt as if a layer of my waking mind had melted away, leaving me relatively worry free. Only, that did not last. Thirty minutes later, I sprung from the bed in a panic, as it felt like the ebb and flow of anxiety began to wash over me. I had such a low tolerance, it felt as if I had gotten too high for my body, and suddenly I was aware of the fact that I was *in* a body. I could feel my body, and I began to get intense thoughts of being unhealthy; it dawned on me that I had not been taking care of myself at all!

I had been eating poorly, rarely exercising, and not getting nearly enough fresh air. My body needed me to care for it if the whole of me was going to function properly.

The whole experience allowed the part of my conscious mind that keeps the everyday worries at the front to momentarily dissipate, and I was left with a very deep knowing of what I needed to do and how I needed to go about doing it. It allowed the core of my own star to expand beyond its limits and begin to see the bigger picture of my own reality. The experience itself felt like it changed me, and I wanted to be sure that I would be able to validate the results of the experience, so I made sure to record it in my magickal journal as soon as I could. Since the date of the experience, I have consistently tried to cut down on consuming dairy (a personal choice), started taking daily walks, and added more daily rituals into my practice. These are small things, but over time they will add up to hopefully make me healthier, and through the record I keep in my journal, I can validate if the initial experience had a positive or negative impact on my life going forward.

When some people think of altered states of consciousness, they may think of psychedelics; for what do psychedelics do better than bring a fresh perspective? I cannot speak to the use of any psychedelic other than cannabis. Years before my experience calling upon the "Angel" in my bedroom, I had experienced the more psychedelic nature of cannabis while consuming a butter that I had stirred into my tea. At the time, I had a migraine and just wanted it to go away. I wasn't expecting anything more than to relieve my pain and go to sleep. Well, I did fall asleep, but I later awoke again in a panic. I began to think I was dying, and I again felt the need to expand out of my body. It felt as if my body was just holding back all of my energy. Then came a wave of knowledge as I laid back on the couch, tossing and turning. I realized that I had been consuming far too much television, and my constant need for social media was not helping me but hindering me. I was too attached to my phone, and I had no sense of freedom beyond the chime of a message or notification that kept reeling me back in. I also remember that at the time I had developed a parasocial relationship with a certain mega-influencer, and it was only through the experience on cannabis that I realized this influencer's message was false. The influencer had been preaching this message that if you weren't on social media you didn't exist; if you didn't have your name on the internet, it would be like you weren't here. How false! We are both here and not here. Yes, we are physically here, and our friends and family know we are here, and they love us. Our dependence on social media plays no part in our worth as a human being. And everything slips through the sands of time, so whether you are or are not on social media really doesn't matter because in the end everything is impermanent. The whole thing lasted about three hours, and I came out of it with a whole new worldview—one that didn't tie my worth to my phone.

Another way of entering into an altered state of consciousness is through physical exercise. Throughout my life, I have had an on-again, off-again love affair with it, but through my magickal practice I found a deeper appreciation for it and the benefits it provides.

I found that at the beginning of starting to move my body again I was excited about the idea of exploring it along with my mind, and I started off with great enthusiasm. I had missed moving my body and taking care of it in that way; I had become very sedentary on behalf of staying home for such a long time and having a great deal of anxiety about going outside alone. (Oddly enough, the act of venturing outside alone has eased the more I have stayed true to my own magickal practice.) I then moved into a period of time where I felt resentful of exercise; I wanted it to end before it even began, and I had a hard time keeping my mind "in the moment." I found myself wanting to rush through it and get to the finish line as if there were some set destination or some prize at the end just waiting to be found.

Once I began to see the connection to what I was doing in my magickal practice, I thought about trying what I had done in my bedroom when I smoked cannabis. That is when I smoked a considerable amount of cannabis before doing thirty minutes of exercise followed by lying on my back in exhaustion. It felt like the pressure had lifted, and I didn't have trouble concentrating. I was not trying to rush the experience but was able to match my breath to my movement and really be there. In the end, I had one of the most beautiful experiences of my life. I began to feel joy rush over me, and my mouth was in a constant smile. I began to laugh, what I now know Terence McKenna would have referred to as "the cosmic giggle."[24] It was then, in that moment, that I realized the illusion of self. Everything that the ego (personality) clings to in order to identify itself in the world is an illusion: fame, money, power, etc. It all gets washed away in the sands of time. We are only here in the moment, and even then, we are impermanent. It felt as if the goal of life was to start a wave that would ripple through time, a wave of love. For the rest of the night, I felt completely blissful, and again I felt like I had an experience that completely changed my outlook and the way I thought of myself and my motivations.

---

24. Terence McKenna, *True Hallucinations: Being an Account of the Author's Extraordinary Adventures in the Devil's Paradise* (San Francisco, CA: HarperCollins, 1993), 112.

The experience felt like a complete change, wave after wave, like a star exploding, such as a supernova. I use this as a metaphor, but what happens in the cosmos is a good metaphor to explain. After the explosion of a supernova, what is left is the core of the star, known as the neutron star. If there is enough mass, this neutron star then becomes a black hole. I believe as individuals when we experience this internal dissolution, we become something new, or, at least, that's the idea that I had. To some, it might matter how an individual gets to the experience, but for me it doesn't matter because the experience itself is so transformative that it stays with you.

Before we leave this chapter, I would like to say that entering into altered states of consciousness does not always require the individual to use a substance; this is one way, but there are many ways. As stated previously, one could use breathwork, meditation, sex, exercise, etc. Art can also be an amazing tool for entering into an altered state of consciousness, almost a trancelike state that would awaken the mind to new ideas, insights, and knowledge.

Confronting your programming means being able to see the patterns that are currently in your life and deciding if they are the right ones. For me, I realized that I had been stuck in a loop of behaviors and ideas, and they weren't serving me or my purpose here. I had to start a whole new loop, one that would allow me to expand. I believe we all have the ability to bring ourselves to the point of singularity where our true self works through us unprohibited. That means that there are many ways to explore your current state of being, and I hope you enjoy the journey.

Chapter 13

PERSONAL POWER

There is a card in the Amenti oracle deck that says, "I keep my own counsel."[25] I've reflected on this card a lot over the past few years, and when I thought about being unapologetically magick, I thought of the card. Keeping your own counsel rests heavily in trusting your own intuition but also in allowing yourself the space to recognize what is best for you without the sound of other people's opinions. One of the things I find myself overcoming again and again in different circumstances is the desire to seek outside counsel. We tend to have this idea that other people might know better than us or have insight into our own lives, but the truth is, if we sit with ourselves long enough, we know the answer.

Building your own counsel means understanding what to do when you need to come up with your own answers. This often looks like peeling back the layers of emotion and getting right down to the core of the issue. For example, I found myself involved in a lot of tech projects, and I began wondering if it was the right space for me. I sent an email to my mentor, and her reply

---

25. Jennifer Sodini and Natalee Miller, "I Keep My Own Council," Amenti Oracle Feather Heart Deck and Guide Book: Ancient Wisdom for the Modern World (RP Studio, 2019).

gave me a general answer about knowing myself. I realized that no one could truly tell me the right thing to do, and I would have to learn to trust myself. I took some time and sat quietly, and I went over the pros and cons and how I felt about the possibilities for my future. I finally concluded that I felt passionate about it for a reason and that I felt my voice could be used in that area. I followed through and found myself making a bunch of new friends and working on some exciting projects, all while learning new things and gaining invaluable experience.

My mentor once told me that part of the spiritual path is finding "where your voice fits the music." I thought that was the perfect metaphor because there have been times when I've tried to fit myself into a certain place and it just didn't feel right. Sometimes you must make your own music. Now, that last part could be debated. Does anything come easy? No, but when you have found your groove, things will start to flow and *feel* easy, despite the obstacles you face. When your voice fits the music, you tend to be able to roll with the punches because you know you're supposed to be there.

Part of finding that place is taking back your personal power. Being unapologetically magick is being able to stand in your own voice and use it. Too often we go through life giving our power away to anyone and everyone without realizing that we are the only ones who can truly give us permission. Part of the issue is that when we look for proof of someone using magick successfully, we look to influencers in the witchcraft space. Yes, many of them are successful and their magick works, but we also forget about the people who live normal lives and have used magick to change their circumstances. Every day people use magick to land their dream job, move to a new location, or create the life they see for themselves. I would argue that magick in that way is much more common than the magick we see practiced by ceremonial magicians, but both have their place and both lead to personal power.

The biggest lesson I have learned so far is that magick is coming to know yourself deeply, and it is challenging, refreshing, and healing. It allows you to stop patterns that aren't serving you and start new ones. It allows you to understand others, and it also gives you the power to help others. When you stand in your power as a witch, you become a beacon for others to do the same. Witches have the power to dream big things and then bring those dreams into reality. They have the power to help others bring their dreams into reality. They offer protection, guidance, and comfort. Being a witch will not always be easy, but I have found it to always be worth it.

Give yourself the room you need to change and grow. Everyone changes; everyone has made mistakes and learned the lessons they needed to. You do not have to be perfect. You do not have to perform that perfection for others. Your power is not something that can be lost; it often just needs to be unearthed. Whether you work with spirits, cast spells, divine with the cards, or read the stars, understand the immense amount of personal power you already have that is only assisted by the use of magick.

TIDAL DISRUPTION EVENT

One day, I started to think about the cosmos and the human spirit and how they might be linked. I thought perhaps that it is true that we are a universe unto ourselves and that we have all parts of that universe within. So just as we are all of the empty space in our birth chart, we are also the black hole at the center of the galaxy. A black hole is formed from the core of a massive star that dies, and when a star gets sucked into a black hole, the star will erupt in what looks like an explosion of light. This is known as a *tidal disruption event.*

Now, before we start thinking that this means something negative, I think it means something more positive that happens internally. I think we have the ability to transform energy perceived as negative into something positive, something that can work for us. We have the ability to absorb the energy, and instead of having it bounce around causing a bunch of havoc in our lives or the lives of others, we can alchemize it.

In Dorothy Morrison's book *Utterly Wicked*, she writes about how if someone sends you negative energy you don't actually have to return it to the sender. You can harness it, transform it, and use it for your own power. She writes, "I explained that all energy—regardless of how it feels—is a gift. It's the very substance from which everything is created. And that being the case, it should never be sent back. Instead, it should be grabbed up, moved and directed, and formed and shaped into something entirely different—something wonderful—something that could be used for personal benefit."[26]

Getting back to the example of a black hole, they can seem scary at first because it appears that all matter is gone, vanished—nothing is left! But within what appears as empty space around the black hole is actually a whole lot of energy that changes over time and manifests itself as pairs of particles. And should a particle and antiparticle pair enter into the black hole's event horizon, sometimes the negative particle will be sucked into the black hole

---

26. Dorothy Morrison, *Utterly Wicked: Hexes, Curses, and Other Unsavory Notions* (Newburyport, MA: Weiser Books, 2020), 99.

and the positive particle will escape.[27] In a way, the positive particle is transformed and does not remain the same as it was before.

There is something powerful about being able to transform energy, and the energy that we look to transform could be our own. At times it can feel like we are our own worst enemies! I know it can for me, as I have a terrible habit of procrastination, but I don't have to wallow in it; I can transform it.

EXERCISE
BLOOMING ENERGY MEDITATION

Dorothy Morrison wrote an excellent spell called "The Swifting of Energy," which can also be found in her book *Utterly Wicked*.[28] I feel that an exercise or spell like that can also be performed mentally, kind of like a meditation. I'd like to offer a mental version to you now.

You will need:
- Nothing but yourself

The steps:
1. Get comfortable and take a deep breath in through your nose, hold it for one second, and exhale slowly out through the mouth.

2. When you are ready, imagine a candle in your mind's eye. Attribute that candle to all of the negative energy you have been feeling, all of the thoughts that aren't helping you, anything you want to transform.

---

27. Nola Taylor Redd, "The Beginning to the End of the Universe: How Black Holes Die," *Astronomy*, Kalmbach Media, February 3, 2021, https://astronomy.com/magazine/news/2021/02/the-beginning-to-the-end-of-the-universe-how-black-holes-die.
28. Morrison, *Utterly Wicked*, 132–36.

3. When finished, in your mind's eye imagine the candle to be lit.

4. Slowly watch as the candle burns down and turns into ash.

5. Take another deep breath in through the nose, hold for one second, and exhale slowly out through the mouth.

6. Now, imagine a seed appears in the ash. It starts to bloom the most beautiful flower you have ever seen! It's gorgeous! This flower represents your transformed energy. It is confidence, strength, gratitude, blessings, and good fortune. It is your energy working for you!

7. When you are ready, take another deep breath in through the nose and out through the mouth. Relax your shoulders, relax your jaw. Know that you are in control.

* * *

Thank you so much for reading through to the last chapter of this book. It means a lot to me to be able to write something like this. I hope that it inspires you to be unapologetically magick. I hope it inspires you to step into your power and to direct the energy and work your magick in the world for something positive.

CONCLUSION

We've covered a lot of ground in this book, a lot of topics that people often fret over, and a lot of decisions to make within one's own personal practice. I do hope that this book has helped you in a small way to be unapologetic about your decision to practice magick, to *be* magick, and to have a little fun doing so. This is the moment when you take what we have discussed and digest it in a way that makes sense for you, adding or subtracting parts as you see fit. The mold cannot be broken because it hasn't yet been made for you; you are unique in every way and so your magick is too. The way you walk through the world, the way your energy speaks and shapes everything it touches, and the way you work with what you call *magick* are all so sublimely and deliciously unique.

You are not a flower to be plucked. You are not a petal that they can pick off and take home with them in their pockets. You are not anyone's toy to be bent into shape at their whim. You are not at the beck and call of anyone else's opinions. You are magick unabashed and unmoved in the face of rejection or shame. You are not the entire ocean; you are the all of every single thing from the sky to the stars to the rocks in the bottom of the sea. You are ever expansive, powerful beyond your wildest dreams, and the savior of your own story.

No one has the right to take away your magick; they couldn't if they tried. No one can tell you that you aren't magick; that, my dear, is simply impossible. No one can tell you exactly how it is supposed to be done. How boring would that be to have everything all figured out? There's much to do, much to explore, much to try and mix and crunch together. Be courageous enough to do so; be bold enough to stand up for yourself against the forces that try to keep you down. Creating your own path can be like walking down a dark forest path; there will be many twists and turns and unexpected things that come out of the trees. It is up to you whether you see it as a frightening journey and one that requires a tour guide, or whether you see it as an exciting adventure with outcomes wildly different than what you would first expect. Magick will take you places you never knew you could go; you will experience things never experienced by others, and you will grow as an individual into parts of yourself you didn't even know existed. It is not for the faint of heart, but it is for the kind of heart, the true of heart, and the strong at heart.

There are many distractions afoot when one begins to take magick seriously; I now see this as one of the greatest tests. If you truly decide to commit yourself to the path of magick, you must be able to stay committed, and perhaps your dedication will be tested through the people, places, and things closest to you. Learn to recognize when the universe is testing you, learn to keep your practice a priority, and you will find that which you have been searching for.

The best teacher you will ever have is yourself; you are, after all, your own guiding force; you are the star you look up to. You are the macrocosm and the microcosm; you are the ship, the captain, the waves, and the beasts in the sea. You are so much more powerful and beautiful and magickal than you give yourself credit for, and I wish for you to see the fullness of it in all of its glory. I wish you success in causing change in conformity with your own will, to feel what it means to make something happen and to move the mountains that others said were impossible.

You are magick, whole, complete, *the* magnum opus. You are unapologetically magick—own it.

REFERENCES

Beyer, Catherine. "What Does Squaring the Circle Mean?" Learn Religions. Dotdash Meredith. Updated January 16, 2019. https://www.learnreligions.com/squaring-the-circle-96039.

Carroll, Peter J. *Liber Null & Psychonaut*. San Francisco, CA: Weiser Books, 1987.

Crowley, Aleister [Master Therion, pseud.]. *The Book of Thoth; A Short Essay on the Tarot of the Egyptians, Being the Equinox, Vol. 3, No. 5*. Artist executant: Frieda Harris. San Francisco, CA: Weiser Books, 2020.

———. *Magick in Theory and Practice*. New York: Dover Publications, 1929.

Greene, Robert. *The 48 Laws of Power*. London: Profile Books, 2000.

———. *Mastery*. New York: Penguin Books, 2013.

Hall, Manly P. *An Alchemist's Primer: Fundamentals of Esoteric Transformation*. Los Angeles, CA: The Philosophical Research Society, 2011.

Hine, Phil. *Condensed Chaos: An Introduction to Chaos Magic.* Tempe, AZ: The Original Falcon Press, 1995.

Hunter, Devin. *The Witch's Book of Mysteries.* Woodbury, MN: Llewellyn Publications, 2019.

Iowa PBS. "George Washington Carver: An Uncommon Life." YouTube video, 56:04. May 8, 2018. https://www.youtube.com/watch?v=_3CVmluYFtI.

Jung, Carl G. *The Red Book: Liber Novus: A Reader's Edition.* Philemon Series. Edited by Sonu Shamdasani. Translated by Mark Kyburz, John Peck, and Sonu Shamdasani. New York: W. W. Norton, 2012.

Lamb, Charles, and Mary Lamb. *Tales from Shakespeare.* By William Shakespeare. Series for the Young. Vol. 7. Leipzig: Bernhard Tauchnitz, 1863.

Lévi, Éliphas. *Transcendental Magic: Its Doctrine and Ritual.* Translated by Arthur Edward Waite. London: William Rider & Son, Limited, 1923.

Martin, Sean. *Alchemy and Alchemists.* Harpenden, UK: Oldcastle Books Group, 2015.

McKenna, Terence. *True Hallucinations: Being an Account of the Author's Extraordinary Adventures in the Devil's Paradise.* San Francisco, CA: HarperCollins, 1993.

McLynn, Frank. *Carl Gustav Jung.* New York: St. Martin's Press, 1997.

Miller, Jason. *Protection & Reversal Magick: A Witch's Defense Manual.* Franklin Lakes NJ: Career Press, 2006.

Moché, Dinah L. *Astronomy: A Self-Teaching Guide*. 4th ed. John Wiley & Sons, Inc., 1993.

Mooney, Thorn. *The Witch's Path: Advancing Your Craft at Every Level*. Woodbury, MN: Llewellyn Publications, 2021.

Morrison, Dorothy. *Utterly Wicked: Hexes, Curses, and Other Unsavory Notions*. Newburyport, MA: Weiser Books, 2020.

Redd, Nola Taylor. "The Beginning to the End of the Universe: How Black Holes Die." Astronomy. Kalmbach Media. February 3, 2021. https://astronomy.com/magazine/news/2021/02/the-beginning-to-the-end-of-the-universe-how-black-holes-die.

Seckler, Phyllis. *The Thoth Tarot, Astrology, & Other Selected Writings*. Edited by David Shoemaker, Gregory Peters, and Rorac Johnson. Sacramento, CA: Temple of the Silver Star, 2017.

Sharp, Daryl. *Jung Lexicon: A Primer of Terms and Concepts*. Toronto: Inner City Books, 1991.

Sodini, Jennifer, and Natalee Miller. "I Keep My Own Council." Amenti Oracle Feather Heart Deck and Guide Book: Ancient Wisdom for the Modern World. RP Studio, 2019.

Sri Swami Satchidananda. *The Yoga Sutras of Patanjali*. Yogaville, VA: Integral Yoga Publications, 2012.

Stevens, Whiskey. *Rise of the Witch: Making Magick Happen Your Way*. Woodbury, MN: Llewellyn Publications, 2021.

St. Pierre, Joellyn. *The Art of Death Midwifery: An Introduction and Beginner's Guide*. San Bernadino, CA: Booksurge, 2020.

TheHighersideChats. "Dr. David Shoemaker | Thelemic Magick, Aleister Crowley, & Finding Your True Will." December 31, 2014. The Higherside Chats. YouTube video, 1:13:47. https://www.youtube.com/watch?v=DaYI3cJlirY.

Wallis Budge, E. A., trans. *The Egyptian Book of the Dead: (The Papyrus of Ani) Egyptian Text Transliteration and Translation.* Garden City, NY: Dover Publications, 2020.

Wolfe, Jane. *Jane Wolfe: The Cefalu Diaries 1920–1923.* Compiled by David Shoemaker. Sacramento, CA: Temple of the Silver Star, 2017.

TO WRITE TO THE AUTHOR

If you wish to contact the author or would like more information about this book, please write to the author in care of Llewellyn Worldwide Ltd. and we will forward your request. Both the author and publisher appreciate hearing from you and learning of your enjoyment of this book and how it has helped you. Llewellyn Worldwide Ltd. cannot guarantee that every letter written to the author can be answered, but all will be forwarded. Please write to:

Whiskey Stevens
℅ Llewellyn Worldwide
2143 Wooddale Drive
Woodbury, MN 55125-2989
Please enclose a self-addressed stamped envelope for reply,
or $1.00 to cover costs. If outside the U.S.A., enclose
an international postal reply coupon.

Many of Llewellyn's authors have websites with additional information and resources. For more information, please visit our website at http://www.llewellyn.com.

NOTES